Breaking the Addiction to Process

An Introduction to Agile Project Management

Breaking the Addiction to Process

An Introduction to Agile Project Management

ELIZABETH SCANLON THOMAS

IT Governance Publishing

IT Governance Publishing
IT Governance Limited
Unit 3, Clive Court
Bartholomew's Walk
Cambridgeshire Business Park
Ely
Cambridgeshire
CB7 4EH
United Kingdom

www.itgovernance.co.uk

© Elizabeth Scanlon Thomas 2011
The author has asserted the rights of the author under the Copyright, Designs and Patents Act 1988 to be identified as the author of this work.

First published in the United Kingdom in 2011
by IT Governance Publishing.

ISBN: 978-1-84928-176-8

PREFACE

More and more IT companies are turning to Agile methodologies because the traditional type of waterfall project development is not working.

Old ways of working can be adhered to as a substitute for thought. For example, in PRINCE2® methodology, there's an emphasis on getting certified and becoming familiar with the thick tomes and multifarious processes that must be followed. This is naturally attractive to government projects and other environments, where there's a temptation to just follow the book and assume that things will come out fine. But if this approach is good, why do so many government projects overrun deadlines and exceed their budgets?

However, there is a another way – and it's called Agile.

You're probably reading this book because your company has decided to use Agile and you need a quick understanding of the subject or you've led a failed project and you're looking for a different way to approach future projects. Or perhaps you're a project leader who wants to try a more innovative approach to your work.

Becoming an Agile company starts with changing the way you and your corporation think about software development. Because that includes breaking the addiction to old-fashioned processes (hiding behind spreadsheets and slides, for example), you can think of this book as a sort of 12-step guide to help you change your mind-set.

Welcome to the flexible world of Agile. You'll never look at project development in the same way again.

ABOUT THE AUTHOR

Elizabeth Scanlon Thomas is a documentation manager at Nokia. She has a BA in English Literature from Stephens College in Columbia, Missouri, and has studied at Cambridge University and done post-graduate work in English and Linguistics at New York University. Elizabeth started out in advertising and marketing, worked as an associate editor for a business magazine then moved into writing for IT. In addition, Elizabeth has had columns published in the *Chicago Tribune* and freelance articles in other magazines. She is a member of the Nokia Agile Community and the London Agile Community. She lives in Reading with her husband and two children.

ACKNOWLEDGEMENTS

Thank you to Kelly Waters and Steve Borthwick for sending me original material to use. Also thanks to my husband for editing and proofing the manuscript.

Thank you also to the following reviewers: ir. H.L. (Maarten) Souw RE, IT-Auditor, UWV; Varinder Kumar, Information Security Officer, ISMS and Infrastructure Management, IRIS Business Services Limited, India; and Antonio Velasco, CEO, Sinersys Technologies.

CONTENTS

Contents

Contents

INTRODUCTION

You've been part of a failed project before. You can remember exactly how it felt – the dawning realisation that you weren't going to make the deadline or that the software wasn't very good. You tried to alert management, but they didn't want to hear. On the contrary, they made public statements about how well the project was going. It seemed surreal that they could be in denial when it was obvious things were going wrong.

Sometimes, management is only too aware that a project is heading for the edge of a cliff, but are unwilling or unable to do anything about it. Instead of trying hopelessly to rescue the project, they concentrate on rescuing themselves. None of them wants to be seen as the cause of failure, so they maintain an attitude of 'The project is going fine – at least, there are no problems in my area.'

Maybe because the project was run in an old-fashioned way, with authoritarian management and little input from workers on requirements or planned functionality, communication in the team was poor. If an employee tried to say anything about the real state of the work, it was seen as being negative and contributing to a sour workplace. 'It's the bad attitude of workers that creates problems,' the deniers would say.

Hidebound companies live behind a façade of truth; that's the inability to say what needs to be said regardless of the impact on the individual or the firm. Organisations demonstrate their aversion to truth by ensuring that what is said is what is expected. In other words, no one is allowed to speak their mind to try and improve the corporate culture because it threatens to destroy the façade and the corporate pretence that everything is fine.

'In my company,' one employee admits, 'it was so bad that my boss began to blame the negativity of the team instead of addressing any underlying reason why we had become so cynical. He told me to speak only in positive terms about my work, the group and our department – even though it was clear we were failing. I felt like a character in an Orwell novel.'

The fear of rocking the boat or losing a job made others not speak up. As the project continued, workers lost heart, muttered about quitting. Moods darkened. Any innovation that would have helped the project was shut down because employees felt unable to speak freely. Information was carefully controlled by management also, leading to a further loss of empowerment to the engineers working on the software.

The project failed because workers knew the truth and management didn't want to admit it. There was no spirit of collaboration or true communication. It was a bad experience, and one that you don't want to repeat now that you are involved in a new project.

Clinging to the old ways

Seeking refuge in old ways of working feels safe, but it's not – your project has a higher chance of failing.

People cling to traditional processes because that's all they know – but there's a new way of thinking (and it requires a change of mind and heart).

There are many reasons for sticking to established methods. For example:

- The belief that the processes can't be changed because that's the way management has decreed it. Often though, this is not the case – the processes have evolved rather than been designed.
- The belief that the processes are there for a reason and trying to change them will lead to chaos.
- Natural resistance to change – reluctance to move out of the comfort zone, the feeling that it's all too difficult, simple fear of the unknown.
- The feeling that it's someone else's responsibility to effect change, especially prevalent in an authoritarian organisation with alienated workers.

Methodologies are adhered to as a substitute for thought.

Let US Defense Secretary Robert Gates explain how successful traditional methodology can be. At the end of one notable government project failure, he commented: 'I would say that what we've gotten for a half billion dollars is an unpronounceable acronym [DIMHRS].'

Introduction

Here's an illustration of how a PRINCE2 project is handled:

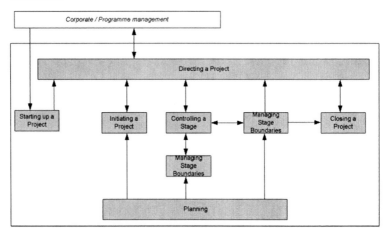

Figure 1: PRINCE2 project

Why do projects fail?

Many projects fail because they are done the conventional way by people or companies who refuse to pursue innovation. (Pause to reflect that Gantt charts and basic project management principles were developed in the 19th century.)

Waterfalls

The traditional way of project management is called 'waterfall', as this type of development is planned up front with no response to changes throughout the life of the project. It's called a waterfall because the phases of the project (requirements, functional specifications and design) are like steps in a waterfall – once one stage is finished, you cascade down to the next level (and by implication can't go back up).

Flexibility is not built into it; so, by the time one of these monster projects is completed, it might not even have produced what the customer wanted (as there's not a lot of communication with them after the planning is finished).

Also in waterfall projects, you don't really do post mortems on what went wrong – a sort of 'lessons learned' process – this makes it more likely that you'll make similar mistakes in future projects.

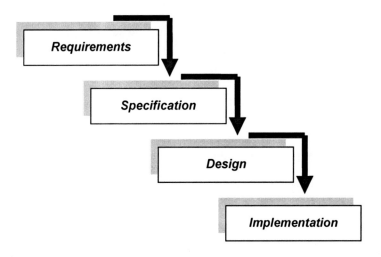

Figure 2: Waterfall project methodology: At the end of each phase, the project spills down to the next level. There is no way back other than restarting

Problems with traditional project management

Problems with the old, established way of project management include:

- No value is gained from the project until it is finished; nothing is released incrementally until the big day.
- No testing is done until the later stages of the project, which means if big problems are uncovered, it's too late to do much about them.
- No approval is sought from customers until the end of the project cycle when their requirements might have changed.
- No changes in plans can happen due to inflexibility of waterfall methodologies.
- If the project manager quits or is replaced, the project is in danger because it might have been too reliant on a single person's direction.

There's a better way to run projects

There is a better way to run projects, though, and that's by using Agile.

More and more companies are turning to Agile development because the traditional type of management is not succeeding.

Agile has evolved through the years from manufacturing processes such as 'just-in-time' (JIT). JIT aimed to reduce waste and over-production by determining which parts were needed by the customer at each stage, rather than mass producing too much product that sat in a warehouse.

JIT came about as a result of the ability to computerise inventory management and predict how many items would be required, where and when. Pre-JIT, large stocks had to be held because no one knew what quantities would be required; running out of something was worse than having too much or too many. After JIT, supplies would arrive just in time to be used. This concept was enlarged and refined until it became useful as a tool for software projects.

Agile is similar to this because software components are delivered as soon as they are ready, rather than being held in stock and being pushed out all in one go.

The basic idea

Here's the idea behind the Agile way of working:

Instead of spending a long time planning a project upfront, then executing the plan without revision or frequent communication with your customer, you plan a small piece of functionality that you can deliver quickly.

The difference with Agile is that you start the project without a complete implementation plan, recognising that the full plan will emerge as you go along. With other techniques, the fact that you have a full plan up front is a weakness, because when a change is necessary there's more to be modified.

You plan the initial piece of work, and select a team who have the skills needed to do it. The idea is that you won't waste time waiting for so-and-so in another part of the organisation to get something done before you can proceed.

As Peter Drucker says, 'The most efficient way to produce anything is to bring together under one management as many as possible of the activities needed to turn out the product.'

You develop a working piece of software (even if it's just a small increment of what the final delivered project will be) and test it as you go along. At the end, you will have something to show the customer, either a prototype or demo.

Often the component will not work in the true sense of the word – rather it will be intended to convey the look and feel of the product.

Then you start the process again working on another increment of the software's eventual functionality.

As you work, you try to reduce the baggage of the project – unnecessary planning too far in advance, for example, or adding functionality that is nice to have, but not really needed (gilding the lily).

Breaking the addiction to process

Because Agile has to start with you changing the way you think and breaking an addiction to old-fashioned processes (hiding behind spreadsheets and slides), you can think of this book as a sort of 12-step guide for you to change your ways of thinking.

Who uses Agile?

Many large companies including IBM, Oracle and Microsoft use Agile methodologies – and more and more smaller organisations turn to Agile each year.

Introduction

Steve Borthwick, Chief Technology Officer (CTO) of Artesian Solutions, explains why his company went Agile:

We are a small software company, 25 people with 10 in development and testing, self funded (I think this has a bearing on our approach to building software). Founded in 2007, this company is my third start-up. We sold the previous one to a big US firm in 2006; so we didn't feel like rookies in the software development business.

I'd had experience of several different development methods over the years and felt for a long time that our development approach was just fine. However, things move on, the technology and people landscape changes. On reflection I was probably stuck in my ways.

Our product could be called 'Web Listening' software; its purpose is to use freely available content on the Internet to accelerate sales and marketing processes in medium to large corporations. Essentially sales and marketing people tell us what they are interested in, and we scour millions of Internet sources like websites, Twitter, blogs, LinkedIn, Facebook and news/RSS feeds. Usually what people want to know about are things like what their prospects and competitors are doing, what the sentiment is regarding conversations about their products, whether there is 'buzz' around their brands or things like health scares which might adversely affect them.

In the early days, we liked to think of ourselves as enlightened developers, but also not at the bleeding edge in terms of development methodology. Our release cycle was around eight months, but we were not a traditional 'waterfall' shop. We built prototypes, used time-boxing techniques and included the business heavily in the design process; a conservative, but iterative approach you could say. However, this approach caused friction in the business for a number of reasons, some technical and some circumstantial, so we decided to change to a more Agile approach last year in an attempt to overcome some of the perceived drag. Initially it was difficult. Our first attempt was a failure, but we persevered and now wouldn't look back.

Trendy is a selling point

'I have to be honest,' Steve continues, 'Agile is trendy, and it is difficult to hire good people without addressing the subject of a modern development method like Agile. On the whole, talented people want to be working on the latest stuff, and if your company is not using it then that's a black mark against you.'

Here's proof that Agile works

Scott Ambler conducts Agile-adoption surveys every year. He reports:

For this survey, a project is considered successful if a solution has been delivered and it met its success criteria within a range acceptable to your organisation, challenged if a solution was delivered, but the team did not fully meet all of the project's success criteria within acceptable ranges (for example, the quality was fine, the project was pretty much on time, but ROI was too low), and a failure if the project team did not deliver a solution at all.

Success Rates survey

According to the 2010 IT Project Success Survey[1], our success rates are:

Ad-hoc projects: 49% are successful, 37% are challenged, and 14% are failures.

Iterative projects: 61% are successful, 28% are challenged, and 11% are failures.

---

[1] Source: *http://www.ambysoft.com*

Agile projects: 60% are successful, 28% are challenged, and 12% are failures.

Traditional projects: 47% are successful, 36% are challenged, and 17% are failures.

Ambler concludes:

Too many traditionalists out there like to use the 'where's the proof?' question as an excuse not to adopt Agile techniques. By providing some evidence that a wide range of organisations seem to be adopting these techniques maybe we can get them to rethink things a bit.

So what are you going to do about it?

Forrester Research concluded in a recent report that Agile is no longer some faddish new theory, but is going mainstream due to the success companies are having with their projects using it. They write:

It's time for software development professionals to stop sitting on the fence where Agile is concerned. According to those who have successfully adopted Agile, the benefits are well worth the effort, and with the recent dramatic increase in Agile adoption, the probability of working in or with an Agile team has increased for everyone.

Shigeo Shingo (one of the architects of Lean Manufacturing) writes:

Are you too busy for improvement? Frequently, I am rebuffed by people who say they are too busy and have no time for such activities. I make it a point to respond by telling people, look, you'll stop being busy either when you die or when the company goes bankrupt.

And don't forget Alvin Toffler:

It is always easier to talk about change than to make it.

The Manifesto for Agile Software Development

The following section is the original manifesto for Agile software development, written in 2001:

We are uncovering better ways of developing software by doing it and helping others do it. Through this work we have come to value:

> Individuals and interactions over processes and tools
>
> Working software over comprehensive documentation
>
> Customer collaboration over contract negotiation
>
> Responding to change over following a plan.

That is, while there is value in the items on the right, we value the items on the left more.

The writers of the Agile Manifesto expanded on these tenets to form 12 principles of Agile. Each principle forms a chapter in this book.

It's up to you to choose the specifics of Agile

Agile methodologies come in different flavours; for example, Kandan and XP. This book gives examples of ways various project managers have handled their Agile projects, but is not meant to be prescriptive.

It's up to you and your company to choose which Agile specifics to use based on what works for you. This book provides an introduction to get you interested and motivated to go Agile. For more details on how to implement Agile in your company, read *Agile Principles Unleashed: Proven approaches for achieving real productivity gains in any organisation²* by Jamie Lynn Cooke.

Get someone to help you

Steve Borthwick explains:

Before we adopted an Agile approach, the most important thing I did was to hire someone who had used it before (an enthusiast) and gave them ownership of the success of the adoption process. Nothing speeds adoption more in my experience than peer-to-peer recommendation. Having an evangelist on the team encouraging everyone was far more effective than top-down (in ignorance) dogma. Of course, you could get the same thing by using a good training vehicle, but having a 'go-to' person in the team worked well.

Without Agile, project failure comes as a complete surprise

Even Agile enthusiasts are quick to point out that Agile doesn't solve all project problems like magic.

Kelly Waters, author of the popular blog All About Agile (*http://www.allaboutagile.com*) comments:

Going Agile takes commitment, tenacity and leadership – it's not fairy dust that you can just sprinkle over your projects and they magically succeed.

I remember when I first got into Agile; I really bought in to the values of transparency, visibility, openness and honesty.

I loved the daily burn-down charts, as they gave me such an early and regular view of a team's progress. My teams proudly stuck the charts on the wall, for everyone to see.

---

² *http://www.itgovernance.co.uk/products/3065*

Now we were not only agile, we were seen to be Agile! But then, I had a high profile project that ran into some problems. Several sprints later and very little was done. My project was screwed. And everyone could see it.

That was stressful. It put a lot of pressure on the team. And it put a lot of pressure on me.

And that's when it struck me ...

The beauty of not doing Agile is that failure comes as a complete surprise, and isn't preceded by months of worry.

Using Agile highlights your problems. And it highlights them early, while there's still time to do something about it.

CHAPTER 1: SATISFY THE CUSTOMER THROUGH EARLY AND CONTINUOUS DELIVERY

Time will not be ours forever.

Ben Jonson

Breaking the Addiction to Process Step 1: Don't be afraid to deliver to customers quickly even if it means living without a full roadmap.

This chapter explains how to work quickly from defining a requirement to delivering a working piece of software to your customer. Instead of time-consuming overall planning ahead of time and working towards a big release, you work on a small piece of the project and deliver that continuously. As Peter Drucker points out, 'Plans are only good intentions unless they immediately degenerate into hard work'.

The failure of traditional project management

You know how people hate to wait to get something big – Christmas is a good example. You're getting a nice present – you'd rather have it now than wait until the 25th December. Customers (stakeholders in Agile) are the same; they don't like waiting either. It makes them nervous. What if they pay your company big money and find out at the very end for the project that what you delivered is not what they wanted or needed? This has been a headache for projects run the old-fashioned way; maybe that's because traditional project management has been around for more than a hundred years.

A little background

The grandfathers of traditional project planning were Henry Gantt and Henri Fayol.

Granddad Number 1: Henry Gantt (1861–1919)

Inventor of the project management tool, the Gantt chart. A Gantt chart is presented like a table where every line represents a task to be done while columns represent the timescale – days, weeks or months.

Here's an example of a Gantt chart:

ID	Task Name	Start	Finish	Duration	2011	2012
1	User requirements	27/01/2011	01/04/2011	47d		
2	Function spec and system design	01/03/2011	01/08/2011	110d		
3	Detail design	01/06/2011	30/12/2011	153d		
4	Build infrastructure	01/08/2011	30/11/2011	88d		
5	Code and test	01/11/2011	29/06/2012	174d		
6	Roll out software	02/07/2012	28/09/2012	65d		

Figure 3: Gantt chart

Gantt charts are easy to read and understood by everyone, which is why they are so persistent in project management. That's their strength. Their weakness is a tendency to depict dates as set in stone – the movement of a milestone on a Gantt chart tends to be seen as failure.

1: Satisfy the Customer Through Early and Continuous Delivery

Granddad Number 2: Henri Fayol (1841–1925)

Creator of the basic project-management functions. He said, 'To manage is to forecast and plan, to organise, co-ordinate and to control.' At the turn of the last century, he said all projects should have these development phases:

* forecasting
* planning
* organising
* commanding
* coordinating
* controlling.

The Scientific Management movement

Both Gantt and Fayol were part of the Scientific Management movement, popular at the end of the 19th and start of the 20th centuries. This held that efficient management should be based on detailed analysis of processes so that they could be more closely controlled, paralleling the then accepted principle of Scientific Determinism.

An atmospheric depiction of determinism was sketched by Charles Dickens in his book *Hard Times*. His character Mr Gradgrind has come to epitomise a man devoted to cheerless profit – a life devoid of any imagination or playfulness. Gradgrind states his aim:

Now, what I want is, facts ... facts alone are wanted in life.

A man of realities. A man of facts and calculations. A man who proceeds upon the principle that two and two are four, and nothing over, and who is not to be talked into allowing for anything over.

1: Satisfy the Customer Through Early and Continuous Delivery

Quantum and Chaos Theory

In the early 20th century, Quantum Theory effectively ended Scientific Determinism. Later (starting in the 1960s) attempts were made to understand this lack of determinism in the field known as Chaos Theory. Agile, following the principle that not everything can be known at the outset, can be seen as a backlash to classical project management in the same way as Chaos Theory was to Scientific Determinism.

John Sullivan comments in a 1989 issue of *The Child and Youth Care Administrator*:

This system involved forecasts from various levels and persons within the organisation. Managers from each level submitted their best estimates of the coming year's activity and, based on this information, the Chief Executive Officer would make up a one-to-five year plan.

In the 1970s, we realised (as we sat in gas lines) that the future was just not going to be a straight-line projection of the past. Planning began to become a very uncertain process as all organisations had to deal with over capacity, resource constraints and volatile markets. Hyper-rational approaches no longer seemed to be the answer.

No one has a crystal ball

The old ways just don't cut it anymore. The world is moving faster than ever, and projects need to be turned around quickly. We need new organisational models for innovation and execution. Our customers don't want to wait around for months or perhaps a year before they see working software.

A senior project manager explains:

1: Satisfy the Customer Through Early and Continuous Delivery

The problem is that requirements are defined at a particular point in time. No one, whether they are a user, an analyst or a project manager, has a crystal ball. Future requirements are very difficult to predict. This is why there is so much emphasis in Agile methodology on delivery of functionality now.

Having an early piece of software helps the customer refine what they want and enables you to understand their needs better. The result is a more successful project.

We need to make a cultural change in companies today from planning to doing and Agile methodology gives us the tools to do it.

An engineer explains how simple it can be:

If you've spent time in the Pacific Northwest, you know of the tyre store empire that is Les Schwab. I remember reading an article a long time ago that said the entire business was built around one simple philosophy: 'Take care of your customers ... take care of your people ... and the bottom line will take care of itself.' Overly simplistic? Maybe. But why not try something that basic if the current business model isn't working?

If you don't get a product out the door fast, your competitors will

In Agile, you learn to live with a rough initial plan that you can start work on immediately (and which you recognise will evolve over time as stakeholder needs change), rather than using up a lot of time trying to plan every last detail of the project upfront.

In traditional waterfall project management, you assemble a team and write a bunch of specifications in advance then stick to that – come what may.

You talk with the customer at first to see what they want, but then it becomes a sort of us-versus-them mentality where the customer wants this or that, but you push back and say it's not what's in the contract, it's not in your remit or you say you can't do everything. 'They are so demanding', you say to each other, 'that soon they'll be wanting us to make their tea for them too.'

When relationships become as tense as this, it's a miracle if any product is built that ends up being what the customer really wants or needs.

So let's talk about Agile, and see if it can help you.

Welcome to the flexible world of Agile

The following section introduces you to Agile concepts and terminology.

Agile vocabulary

Here is a list of the Agile vocabulary you'll need to know as you read the rest of the book.

Completed experiences should be demonstrable to customer or prototyped.

Epic	Highest-level requirement element. An epic is divided into lower-level requirements: Experiences and Enablers. It is planned to be released in a certain timebox, but development can take longer than that.
Experiences	Experiences are easy to understand by the consumer (for example, 'As a customer, I want a mobile phone that is easy to use.')

Experiences are similar to requirements in traditional project management. Completed experiences should be able to be demonstrated to customer or prototyped.

Enablers   Enablers are technical features needed to implement Experiences.

Product backlog   Prioritised list of user stories (requirements).

Daily scrum   Short stand-up meeting. What did you do? What will do today? What is blocking you?

Scrum master   Leads the daily scrum. Tracks work completed and remaining, and organises removal of things blocking the team.

User stories   User stories are like traditional requirements, but expressed in sentences from the customer perspective ('As a customer, I want a mobile phone that's easy to use.')

Timebox   A year (approximately) of the project is called a timebox. This roughly equates to a traditional software product release.

Train   A timebox is broken down into trains (sometimes referred to as an Experience Development Train (EDT)). A train lasts approximately 8 to 10 weeks.

Sprint	A train contains sprints. Sprints last about two weeks and are designed to be able to produce potentially shippable code or a demo for a stakeholder, or perhaps just a prototype. (Sprints are what Agile terms 'iterations'.)
Sprint tasks	The lowest level of functionality a team can work on. User stories are broken down into tasks and worked on during a sprint.

Delivering in increments

In the world of Agile, project management is less rigid than you're used to. You have a team, like before, but instead of working for perhaps a year for one huge delivery of software, you break the functionality down into do-able parts that you can give to the customer continuously (the overall project can still take a year, but by the time you get there, you will have delivered several increments of the software already). These little parts of functionality (requirements) are called user stories and should be defined by the customer.

Iterative development

The main thing to keep in mind is that Agile is iterative – whereas a traditional project will start and end in a year and deliver something big, Agile works in cycles of two weeks (a sprint) with three to four sprints in a train and a few trains in an epic that is time-boxed to a year – the idea is to get something done in that two weeks that the customer can see, and build on that as the project continues. Agile is implemented by scrum teams.

A collection of user stories (experiences and the enablers needed to make that experience work – such as changes to platform code so an application can run in the background, for example) is bundled into a train on an epic project.

Decide who owns the product or the epic

The product owner is ultimately responsible for the software.

The epic is the highest level of requirements. An epic shows the scope of the work you want to do.

As the epic project covers both experience and enabler development, both experiences and enablers can be referred as 'experiences' for shorthand.

Collect user stories (requirements)

User stories not completed in the first sprint become your product backlog.

All the user stories (requirements, but from the customer's point of view, not yours) your team needs to complete are collected into a product backlog (a list of user stories in order of importance). Each requirement in the backlog is given levels of importance, such as Must Do or Nice to Have – that way you know which requirement you can dump if time gets short or some complication happens that means you can't get everything done that you'd planned.

Stories belong in sprints and underneath that are sprint tasks – the smallest unit of software you can do. Once you decide to take a user story into a sprint and do it, the team breaks the work down further into smaller sprint tasks, then get to work on that for the next two weeks.

Define your scrum team

Assemble a self-managed team of motivated engineers.

To do the work for an epic, you assemble a scrum team with all the expertise you need (you can't have an important piece of work in the epic that has to be done by someone else who has a different agenda, for example – it all has to be within the one team). The scrum follows a certain set of behaviours; for example, there is a short stand-up meeting every day where you work to remove any obstacles. It's led by a scrum master.

Break work down into shippable increments

Each sprint results in potentially shippable code.

The scrum team works in a sprint. The sprint lasts approximately two weeks long, and its aim is to produce some working piece of software that the customer can have or it can be demonstrated to them. The whole idea of Agile is to get something out of the door quickly, that can be continuously tested and integrated into the main software, and problems can be caught and rectified early on.

Agile works in iterations so once you complete your first sprint, you start the cycle all over again. Each sprint produces more and more working code. You build on these project increments (using sprints) until the whole thing is done.

1: Satisfy the Customer Through Early and Continuous Delivery

Get code or a demo out to the customer fast

The train leaves the station on time, even if not all the passengers (your user stories) are on it.

Sprints are contained within a train. When you hear someone on an Agile team ask another person: 'Which train are you on?', they aren't talking about public transport. They are trying to determine where in the development cycle that person is working. (Different groups in a company are working on different functionality or platforms so have their own epics and trains.) A train contains several sprints and can last for 8 to 10 weeks.

The metaphor of the train in Agile is used because:

- Trains leave on schedule (fixed project dates).
- Trains can contain only so much cargo (user stories or requirements are passengers on the train).

Done is done

You can't say your work is finished until the customer's Definition of Done is done.

A timebox has a fixed end date, and the epic can't be declared finished until the Definition of Done is met. (This definition of done is set by the stakeholders – your customers.)

Decide on a project completion date

An Agile project is in a timebox. The timebox finish date should remain stable, no matter what happens in the sprints.

1: Satisfy the Customer Through Early and Continuous Delivery

An epic should be completed within a certain timebox (corresponds to a big release in traditional projects). A rule of thumb is one timebox per year that contains several epic projects.

It's a little more complicated than that

Of course, Agile is more complicated than outlined in this overview. The purpose of this book is to give you a taste of Agile, and to tell you about the change of heart and mind it requires for you to become a successful practitioner.

Crisis calls for a different approach

Kelly Waters discovered Agile at a time of complete crisis. He explains:

We'd won a big project. We were elated – it was by far the biggest deal we had ever done, worth several million pounds over a few years. Then the problems started. The supplier we had suddenly put his price up from £112k to £1.3 million. We decided we'd rather spend a million developing it ourselves than pay that ransom.

Then the existing supplier terminated with only three months' notice. So now – instead of a £112k customisation in 6–12 months, we had just 3 months to do a £1m complete rebuild. We found an external partner to work with, but they said the project was impossible to do using a traditional approach. We decided to overlap all the project phases, so we could get the work out faster.

They called the way we did this project Agile. We managed our work in a very lightweight way and in timeboxes. The project was stressful, but a huge success. We worked crazy hours, but we did it.

1: Satisfy the Customer Through Early and Continuous Delivery

But the whole project, because it had been Agile, was strangely enjoyable. We hadn't been bogged down with process. So, despite the extreme circumstances, everyone was happy. That's how I discovered Agile.

CHAPTER 2: WELCOME CHANGING REQUIREMENTS

There is no greater hell than to be a prisoner of fear.

Ben Jonson

Breaking the Addiction to Process Step 2: Stop making rigid requirements in advance then being afraid to change them.

Some managers are afraid of changing project plans because:

- You'll be seen as a wimp because you don't have a 'consistent vision'.
- You think you need to keep a tight grip on everything around you.

Often, though, the 'vision' will be incorrect in the first place, and the 'control' is illusory. These are two important reasons why authoritarian management styles usually fail.

If you really knew somehow what your customer would need by the end of the project cycle, or what products your competitors would release in the middle of your work, maybe this old-fashioned view of good leadership would hold. But not these days – not when the world can change overnight.

Remember the words of Helmuth von Moltke (1848–1916), chief of staff of the Prussian Army:

No plan survives contact with the enemy

You might as well *welcome changing requirements* in a project cycle, because they'll be forced on you anyway if you're listening to the changing needs of business. And if you're not listening, your competitors will be and it will be they who end up with your customers.

Also, what if you do the entire planning upfront, freeze the requirements then one of the following events occurs?

- The stakeholder realises that they missed a feature in the initial planning.
- A bug is in the software. That has to be planned for.
- The stakeholder realises they asked for the wrong thing. The product you're working on isn't what they really need.
- A management change happens at the top of the company so the product priorities have changed.
- New legislation has been introduced that requires a change in the product.

It's best to admit that variation in a roadmap will occur and plan for that.

One CEO admitted:

My company was too slow. I had to go for more speed to make decisions and launch our products faster on to the market. My goals were:

- to be quick enough to adapt to market variation
- to be more focused on customer needs and results
- to better understand our competition, so we can beat them
- to be obsessed with hardware and software excellence

- to loosen the gears to make things happen within the company
- to give more flexibility to local groups and departments to speed up decision making.

This CEO realised that his hidebound way of looking at the universe was actually holding his company back. There's nothing like a bad bottom line to foster the comprehension that change is needed.

This is the way it used to happen

In the old mode of working, managers drew a line at some point and said these things will go in at the release – once things below the line are out, they aren't done at all.

That meant they would be put in the next release, which might be a year away. Decisions about what to put in might have been driven not by how important the requirement is, but by how easy it is. Everything was driven by system design, not by requirements.

In a conventional project, all phases had to be signed off before the next one could start. For example, the user requirements document had to be completed then the functional specification was written. Only after that was done did a team start on the actual system design.

Once you had a system design, you decided on the technologies to use and then worked on the detailed design to explain how the functionality would be implemented.

There also the problem that no one has perfect knowledge of requirements at the beginning. If you add to that the fact that you're trying to hit a moving target anyway, because requirements change all the time, then it makes it doubly important to be able to incorporate changing requirements as they become apparent.

Planning in an Agile world

In Agile methodology, change is the one steady thing in a project. So it's understood that the first plan you release for a project will be rough. It must be detailed enough only to get your team started. In Agile projects, you plan continuously, and correct any veering off course as you go along. You plan through backlogs and burn-down charts, not through Gantt and PERT charts.

Define user stories then implement them

First of all, you have a stakeholder who wants something produced. Someone has to own this work – that's where the product owner comes in. The product owner and other stakeholders decide what items need to be developed into a finished product or software delivery. Those items are the requirements, or in Agile parlance, user stories.

In planning for a release, you and your team must decide which user stories need to be done first. Break them down into do-able tasks – the smallest unit you can so it can be delivered to a customer rapidly – and determine which ones must be done first. (Hint: pick the easiest thing first. Your team will be more motivated if it develops something quickly to show the customer, and the customer is pleased with progress early on in the game.)

Planning how long it will take

The duration of Agile projects or sub-projects can be measured in the ways listed below. You can use whatever system of measurement that meets your specific needs.

- **Timebox = 1 year**
  This would have equated to a traditional software product release cycle.

- **Train = 8 to 10 weeks**
  A timebox is broken down into trains.

- **Sprint = 2 weeks**
  A train contains sprints and each should produce potentially shippable code, a demo for a stakeholder or perhaps a prototype.

These are rough estimates, of course. You decide how long you need for each element, but it is a good idea for a timebox to have a fixed end for your team to work towards.

How is Agile planning implemented?

The actual planning is done in scrum teams. Scrum teams are made up of specially selected engineers who are self-motivated and who you can trust to competently do the work.

What a sprint contains

A sprint starts with the product backlog. That's a list of prioritised requirements.

User stories (requirements from the stakeholders' point of view) evolve during development, so you must be prepared for an ever-changing environment.

Units of functionality in Agile: user stories and sprint tasks

The scrum teams work to develop items on their product backlogs (a list of user stories, bugs and features that need to be done). User stories can be broken down still further into sprint tasks, the smallest unit of functionality.

Product backlog

The master list of everything you need to do on a project is the product backlog. To produce your first backlog, make a list of everything that you can think of that needs to be done. This list can be a rough draft. As you may remember, Agile is about having work in progress that can be changed quickly as the marketplace or a customer's needs evolve over the project's life cycle.

Once you have a backlog, keep it simple and do the easiest thing first. That will build the confidence of your team and give you some momentum as well.

User stories are Why not What

In the old days, a company had a contract to do this or that functionality so requirements used to be What. But in Agile, user stories are Why. For example, an Agile user story could be 'I want to be able to make calls in Waterloo station but not be overheard by anyone next to me'. In a traditional project, this requirement could have been, 'The phone call must be of a decibel level of x.' When you write down what the customer wants their consumer to experience, you avoid the specification aspect of it. This should also help motivate engineers more to do the work, as they are free to implement their own solutions to problems rather than being told what to do.

Writing user stories

Kelly Waters has some advice for writing good user stories:

User stories are a simple way of describing features or user requirements. The basic construct is this:

As a [PARTICULAR TYPE OF USER], I want to […], so I can [WHATEVER]

This simple outline helps people to express user requirements consistently and in a very simple way. In a short statement, you know who wants it, what they want and why. That's a lot of information, in a very concise format.

User stories are listed on your product backlog. In the sprint, they are represented on postcards or Post-its to be tracked on the whiteboard. You know your stories are too long if they don't fit on a postcard.

On the back of the card, you can write test confirmations, or otherwise, how you will know that it works?

User stories should be independent and negotiable. They are reminders, not a fixed contract. They enable you to capture requirements piecemeal, one feature at a time.

After using user stories, I find it hard to imagine ever working with a functional specification again.

Example: user stories[3]

This section gives you examples of user stories that demonstrate Agile principles in a non-software-specific way.

- As a host, I want my friends to know about the event, so that they will come.
- As a host, I want to know about my friend's likes/dislikes, so I can decide what to prepare.
- As a host, I want sufficient and varied side dishes for all the guests, so that no one is bored with the selection.
- As a host, I want there to be enough drinks for my guests, so that the reputation of my parties is maintained.
- As a host, I want to be able to give my guests barbecued food for lunch, so I can cook everything outside.
- As a driver, I want some choices of non-alcoholic drinks, so I can drive home safely.
- As a vegetarian guest, I'd like to have some choices, so that I can eat more than potato salad.
- As a neighbour, I don't want to be disturbed late at night, so that we keep good relationships in the street.
- As a guest, I want to dance (badly) to cheesy 80s hits, so I can enjoy myself.
- As a host, I want my guests to be able to continue to use the garden after dark, so that we have enough space for everyone.
- As a host, I want a quick clean-up operation the following day, so I can mow the lawn.

---

[3] User stories by Alistair Wharton from Nokia

2: Welcome Changing Requirements

In a sprint, a team takes a user story and tries to develop it. The user story is broken down into sprint tasks. Here's an example of sprint tasks using one of the earlier user stories.

As a host, I want to be able to give my guests barbecued food, so I can cook everything outside

A scrum team has chosen to implement this story. They can't actually do it easily – it has to be broken down into smaller increments called sprint tasks. Here's how that user story breaks down into more manageable tasks for a sprint:

- Find BBQ, evict spiders and clean off last year's grunge.
- Obtain sufficient fuel for the day.
- Determine BBQ site and clear up the area.
- Buy meat from the butchers.
- Marinate meat overnight.
- Light the BBQ in good time.
- Pre-cook meat (pork and chicken) to avoid poisoning people.
- Cook meat to be ready between 12:00 and 15:00.
- Clean up and pack away BBQ.

The Moscow Method for setting priorities

One way to determine the priority of requirements is the Moscow method. (The 'o' letters are only in there to make it an acronym – it's really MSCW.)

In the old days, projects tried to get every single requirement done; in Agile, the scope of the project changes, therefore prioritising your work is essential.

All requirements are important, but you can't do them all – some of them have to be completed urgently, while others can be delayed or put off indefinitely. The Moscow method enables you to put a priority on each item in your backlog. Assign each of them one of the following priorities:

M Must have requirement
S   Should have if at all possible
C   Could have but not critical
W Won't have the time to do it now, but maybe later.

Do the essential requirements first. Prioritising your workload goes a long way to increasing efficiency.

How fast can your team work? It depends on their velocity

Release planning in Agile must take into account a scrum team's velocity. The velocity is made up of how many members there are to the scrum team, how complex the items to be done are, and the number of user stories to be done in the sprint (approximately two weeks of time). So basically velocity means: how many tasks (on average) can your team get done in a single sprint? (Sprint tasks are the smallest unit of a user story.) Your judgement is based on previous sprints – how much did you get done in an earlier iteration? Use this as a basis for judging how much you can get done in future sprints.

When do requirements change?

During sprints when you start to build software, you find things missing – gaps that need to be filled with new user stories – or you'll discover that user stories you thought you could do are too large and need to be broken down.

It could also be that a requirement you thought was necessary really isn't and can be removed from the sprint.

The point is that a project's user stories evolve over time, and you must be flexible enough to react and respond.

The difference between this view of changing user stories and the traditional one is stark. As a project manager explains:

In a conventional project, changed requirements mean going back to the drawing board, starting the project all over again because there is no easy way within the constraints of the methodology to incorporate revised specifications.

What would have to happen is that the requirements would have to be updated, then the functional spec, and these things would all have to be signed off. Then the designs would have to be updated and only then could the deliverables be changed.

Tasks are estimated collaboratively

Because Agile removes the need for you to sit down and plan a project out by yourself, without enough input from others to make it realistic, there are a few ways to make planning more fun and productive at the same time.

Old modes of management are rigid and over-formal, but new methodologies, such as Agile, can add a playful aspect to project management. In fact, the initial project planning in Agile is referred to as 'the planning game'.

You can, of course, sit down in a meeting room and talk to determine which user stories will go into a sprint, but in Mike Rhodes' group at Nokia, planning is done by playing Planning Poker.

Mike plays Planning Poker with his team in each sprint planning meeting. The cards have numbers on them based on the Fibonacci sequence. In the Fibonacci sequence, the first two numbers are 0 and 1, and each subsequent number is the sum of the previous two (thus 0, 1, 1, 2, 3, 5, 8 and so on).

A set of cards based on the Fibonacci sequence works well for an exercise of this type because there are a large number of small values and relatively fewer large values (that is, if you limit the highest number to a finite number – for example, 100). This reflects the range of values for length of steps in a project, which typically have many short operations together with a few large ones.

The scrum master (equivalent to a team leader in traditional project management) picks a user story (requirement), reads a description and asks if anyone has a question. Next, they ask for someone to pick a number from the Planning Poker set for how long they think it will take to implement the requirement. Just asking someone to do that usually prompts more questions about the requirement, and that gets information flowing in the team.

At the end of this exercise, everyone shows the cards they've picked that show their estimates for how long the project tasks will take. The person with the highest number is questioned first: for example, why did you pick 13? That provokes more discussion. People take their cards back until there is some agreement: when people are showing the same type of cards, you can see some consensus is being reached.

Mike Rhodes says:

If people choose a big number, it has a bigger variance on it. Accuracy planning is more percentage than an actual variation – if you choose a smaller number, you are more likely to be accurate. If you think something is going to take one day, for example, it will probably take between two and four days to complete. But if you choose 20, it could be between 30 and 50 days to complete. So the rule in Planning Poker is if people pick numbers above 20, we have to take the requirement and break it down into a smaller work item. The objective of accurate Agile planning is to break requirements down until they can be done in a sprint of two weeks.

When others in the group disagree about an estimate you made for an amount of work to be done, that's good because you then discuss the assumptions behind how many days you thought it would take to do the work versus what, for example, Sue thought. If Sue has more in-depth knowledge about a problem in this area than you do, you will hear her viewpoint and learn from it.

It is very likely that some estimates will differ significantly. If estimates differ, the high and low estimators explain their estimates. It's important that this does not come across as attacking those estimators. Instead, you want to learn what they were thinking about.

As an example, the high estimator may say, 'To test this story, we need to create a mock database object. That might take us a day. Also, I'm not sure if our standard compression algorithm will work, and we may need to write one that is more memory efficient.' The low estimator might respond, 'I was thinking we'd store that information in an XML file – that would be easier than a database for us. Also, I didn't think about having more data – maybe that will be a problem.'

Both experienced and inexperienced programmers can take part in the poker game. You don't have to assign tasks to everyone in Planning Poker – basically you're trying to foster understanding of the complexity of the project by clarifying the tasks and identifying risks.

Don't forget that any tasks you plan to complete during the sprint also have to have tests created for them too, which can sometimes take as much effort as writing the original code. Also, the numbers in Planning Poker are only relative; it doesn't mean you can only spend one day doing something just because you selected a card with the number one on it.

It's essential to get the backlog right

Kelly Waters warns that it is essential to get your backlog correct:

I have found time and time again, if your product backlog is wrong, you run into all sorts of problems.

The product backlog is a list of all the things you want to get done on the product. As far as possible, the backlog should be user oriented. It should include a list of experiences (features), not tasks.

Features should be described in business language and be understandable by anyone. They should be listed in priority order, as prioritised by the product owner. The most valuable experience should be at the top; the least valuable at the bottom.

There is no longer any reason to say no. Just ask 'where does it fit on this list?'

The product backlog is key to managing expectations, and focusing the team on the right priorities. In my opinion, it's imperative you get the product backlog in order before proceeding further with your implementation of scrum.

In the past, I didn't, and my project paid the penalty for it.

Why we went Agile

Steve Borthwick of Artesian Solutions outlines the main frictions caused by his company's old development approach which then resulted in the entire company going Agile:

I forgot why I asked for that – A lengthy development cycle meant that as our ideas and products evolved there was a long period in between someone asking for something and us being able to deliver it, even if the request was trivial. Often the sponsor of the idea lost interest or found a different way or simply forgot why they asked for it. Sometimes it meant the difference between acquiring or losing a new client who had been sold on the promise of some new functionality.

Ask for cash, more often – Being a self-funded company meant that we had to earn money almost from day one and maintain a cash flow that kept the lights on and the servers running as the product filled out and matured. This means quick deliverables that can be sold; that is, demonstrable and that work. An eight-month cycle between releases was causing drag on the rate of growth of the business and pressure on the developers to cut corners and release things prematurely. The business hated the idea that they would need to wait months for that simple little feature they wanted that may make a big difference to a particular sales engagement.

Big releases means big testing – When you have a small team that crams six months of development into a single release, testing it is a nightmare. Even with reasonably good unit test coverage, it's still onerous. Regression testing after the first release was not easy, simply because of the volume of work. For a small team, it becomes unrealistic to do it in one big hit fairly quickly.

Oh yeah, I forgot to tell you, we're not doing that anymore – Progress reporting was difficult and caused friction because problems were not communicated up the chain until it was too late to do anything about them. Software development is difficult to estimate, particularly when you are building something you've never built before. It is especially difficult when you are a very small team who cannot afford the luxury of having completely specialised roles – for example project managers, product managers, QA, support and so on. It becomes very easy to get two or three decision steps away from the path of the original business goal without an easy way for everyone to realise it.

There are a lot of (expensive) ways to skin a cat – With an eight-month cycle we would typically have weekly (or fortnightly) meetings. However, the meetings were more like management updates rather than a forum for the developers to actually find out what was going on at a peer level. Often similar features would be built by two different people because they had no proper visibility of what anyone else was working on. Similarly, people would get stuck and sit on the problem when the person at the next desk had already solved a similar problem.

He who shouts loudest – Without a formal system for recording feature requests and prioritising them, it was typical that we only built whatever the most recent client wanted rather than a balance of new features across all clients. This often doesn't become entirely apparent until you get a client who shows reluctance to renew their contract, by which time you have to adopt a reactive mode rather than a preventative one (always stressful). Having a feature tracking system is not necessarily an attribute exclusive to Agile projects, but the emphasis on maintaining a formal product backlog is a key part to greasing the wheels of subscription renewal.

Friction makes things hot, hot things burn you – One of the biggest lessons we had to learn was that, unless you can make the development process as smooth as possible, then Agile is hard to make work. Rapid releases and continuous change has a cost, and that cost is amplified painfully unless you are in control. Automated and, most importantly, integrated systems to take the load off keeping track of everything that's going on are critical to the success of the approach. It would probably be possible to do this on paper, but it would certainly be less smooth and more stressful.

Steve adds:

2: Welcome Changing Requirements

My main concern about Agile was the strong emphasis on short release cycles; it seemed logical that features, that is, the ones too big to fit in one sprint might simply never get done and that we might be unable to resist the temptation to continually add features to an on-going sprint making it longer and longer as it progressed.

I was worried about having too many meetings, I didn't want us to end up like a 'talking shop' giving developers an excuse not to progress or simply slow them down with unnecessary chat.

I continue to be concerned that short-release cycles make product management lazy: the temptation is to neglect detailed design because the feeling is that you'll see something soon anyway and it can be changed then. This might be OK for smaller features, but can be disastrous for larger ones where getting the underlying architecture right is critical and expensive to fix afterwards. Using design patterns like dependency injection and insisting on a good clear separation of concerns is essential in minimising the potential impact of this.

We were a little fearful of change. Our existing iterative approach had delivered good products in the past; we all understood it and more importantly the management were tuned into the rhythm of it. We also understood the friction it caused, but this also meant that outcomes were more predictable, if not always desirable. An Agile approach with even more emphasis on iteration is clearly an all-or-nothing proposition – it would be difficult to just adopt a small part of it and it would probably fail unless the whole organisation was behind it. Change always represents a risk–reward balance and for a small organisation this balance is even more critical to get right.

Some key principles have been hammered out which seem to help, these are:

Timeboxing needs to go hand-in-hand with each sprint; this is really hard to do as everyone thinks their pet feature should be done first. The main reason our first sprint failed was that we loaded more and more things into it under pressure from the business; it ended up taking three months, not hugely different from before.

Strong management and commitment from all parties is required to keep the sprint times short; eventually if you succeed then the business gets more comfortable implementing the timebox since they are confident that the features dropped will simply appear in the next release only a few weeks away. My new mantra is 'change is only a few weeks away', not quite true in all cases, but the sales guys like it.

Stand-up meetings need to be snappy and they need to be managed so that people don't simply repeat the same old stuff over again; pointed questions need to be asked and a little bit of tension seems to be a good thing.

Steve summarises:

Change is the only constant in software development and it should be embraced, but embraced with caution. Change for change's sake is not profitable.

There is a difference between changing the way you do things, so it enables you to tackle something new and to sell more software, and changing something that works so that the code is more elegant, but nobody notices. A more important change vector is the change occurring in the world of your customer; if you can adapt quickly to take advantage of changes in their world, then you will end up with happier customers and more useful software.

CHAPTER 3: DELIVER WORKING SOFTWARE FREQUENTLY

In small proportions we just beauties see;

And in short measures, life may perfect be.

Ben Jonson

Breaking the Addiction to Process Step 3: Stop overwhelming yourself with all you have to do – break tasks down into increments and do the smallest things first.

Do you leave things to the last minute, then feel like you'll sink from the boatload of stuff you have to do? Agile methodology has a way to handle this that will help you in real life too.

Have you ever seen one of those Lazy Person's Guide to Getting Things Done-type of article? The generic items on those lists are applicable to an Agile project too, for example:

- **Make a To Do list**. Keep a notebook with you and cross out any item you've completed. Bask in the feeling of accomplishment of getting something done.
- **Stop putting things off**. Get up every day and do something, no matter how small. Once you've done a small thing, the big things won't seem so enormous.
- **Set priorities**. What do you really have to do first? Can something be done later? Can you not do it at all? You can't do everything all at once. Decide what to work on first, and what can wait.

- **Set a time limit on how much you'll work on items.** This is a good principle borrowed from Cognitive Behavioural Therapy. You can become overwhelmed if you think 'I have such a big job ahead of me doing x; it's too much; I can't even get started on it.' Instead, tell yourself that you'll only spend 30 minutes working on it, not a minute more or less. The thought that you only have to do a dreaded task for 30 minutes then you can go off for a tea break makes the task less onerous. You will often find you work past the time allotted because you are enjoying the achievement of working towards your goal.

- **Get rid of distractions**, or rather management should lessen them for scrum team members. Engineers should be able to work without too many meetings, or being burdened with tasks that aren't related to coding. A scrum master has to keep working on removing obstacles from the rest of the team, so they can get on with their tasks.

It's common sense, right? So is Agile. As in the list above, you break big jobs down into increments, so they are easier to do. If you do the simplest thing first, you get a sense of accomplishment and motivation that will carry you on to finish harder, more complex tasks.

Produce code increments during a sprint

The idea behind a sprint is to always have something to show for the work the team has done at regular intervals – that makes tracking progress easier and the customer can give you earlier feedback.

How it works

Once you've broken down your project's requirements into smaller chunks of requirements or user stories (which are kept in the product backlog), you decide which of these user stories you will complete in a sprint.

The user story that your team does in a sprint is broken down further into sprint tasks. Each member of the scrum team chooses a task to work on.

Sprints are usually two-week cycles where your team tries to produce a small piece of working code to show the customer. Once a sprint is done, the team can demo the code to the stakeholder or show them a prototype. Four to five sprints can be contained within one train.

Mike Rhodes, a senior manager at Nokia and an Agile coach, comments:

Working in sprints means you can vary the size of your team to accommodate the workload you have. Some large companies have their sprints coordinated, and they can change the team size. At regular intervals, all the scrum masters throughout the company come together to talk about the various projects going on and discuss the best way to allocate resources.

Ideally, Mike says, teams should stay together for at least six months to learn to work together and gel.

Sprints are iterative work cadences that help project teams and management deal with the unpredictability of creating software.

How to get started in a sprint

Each person in the team picks one of the sprint tasks to work on. They pick their own work; the manager cannot assign work to them.

Team members decide how to get the tasks done during the sprint.

Work progress is updated in daily stand-up meetings called scrums.

Sprints have to be of equal time; you can't have a sprint of two weeks then one of ten weeks, for example. That's not really a sprint, that's more of a milestone from PRINCE2 methodology.

How much work has your team done?

You can see how much your team has achieved in each sprint by creating a burn-down chart. A burn-down chart is a graphical representation of the information on your team's whiteboard. A whiteboard is an essential team tool for Agile and its use is explained more fully later.

Basically, your team writes down tasks it must do on Post-it® notes and places them on a whiteboard. Items placed on the left on the board aren't done, and the ones on the right side are finished. That gives you the information you need to produce a burn-down chart.

Steve Borthwick shares an example of one of his company's burn-down charts and explains how they work:

Our workflow tool spits out actual data and our source code control system links the tickets in our workflow system to code commits.

Here's an example:

Date	Day	Burn (FPoints)		Tracking		
		Plan	Actual	Plan	Actual	Committed
22/09/2010	1	12	1	222	233	1
23/09/2010	2	18	10	204	223	10
24/09/2010	3	11	0	193	223	0
27/09/2010	4	4	12	189	211	12
28/09/2010	5	5	19	184	192	19
29/09/2010	6	9	20	175	172	20
30/09/2010	7	10	8	165	164	8
01/10/2010	8	17	2	148	162	2
04/10/2010	9	20	1	128	161	1
05/10/2010	10	18	2	110	159	2
06/10/2010	11	6	3	104	156	3
07/10/2010	12	11	2	93	154	2
08/10/2010	13	7	34	86	120	34
11/10/2010	14	14		60	#N/A	#N/A
12/10/2010	15	12		50	#N/A	#N/A
13/10/2010	16	12		35	#N/A	#N/A
14/10/2010	17	12		20	#N/A	#N/A
15/10/2010	18	7		10	#N/A	#N/A
18/10/2010	19	11		5	#N/A	#N/A
19/10/2010	20	18		0	#N/A	#N/A
	Tot	234	114	0	0	

Figure 4: Workflow tool output

Steve comments:

This isn't 100 per cent perfect, but it gives me enough visibility to gauge the health of each sprint. I plug this data into a little spreadsheet every now and then and hey presto, there's my burn-down rate.

An example of the resulting burn-down chart follows:

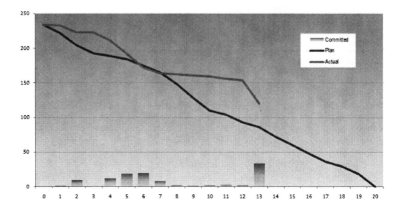

Figure 5: Burn-down chart

He explains:

The Y axis is something we call 'function points', which is an abstract measure of complexity applied to 'tickets', that is, a chunk of work that someone needs to do. I find using an abstract value like this rather than 'days' works better – different people have different day rates depending on skill and experience.

The X axis is the working day number in the sprint (that is, a four-week sprint) – what we see in the burn-down chart is the summary level.

Steve comments on the metrics his company uses in the charts:

This is important for the rest of the business to buy into; as in most other fields, harder work or more hours are the measures to watch.

Ideally, you need to come up with some measures that correlate to the 'usefulness' of your product. In our case, we have such measures and they centre on the 'relevance' of the content we deliver; the tracking mechanisms are built into the product itself so the measurement is fairly straightforward.

Sprint retrospective

It's important after a sprint to review what you did and see where you went wrong, so the next sprint will be more productive and efficient.

You can more easily judge if a sprint was a success or a failure if you run automated testing. Potentially shippable code needs a way to be rapidly tested, so you need an automated test suite. Creating 'testware' is a vital part of any sprint where code is being engineered that is going to be demonstrated to the customer afterwards.

Grading the sprint

Sprints should be defined as Pass/Fail – if something remains undone or didn't work, the sprint fails. Mike Rhodes, however, describes a sprint as a success, even if something went wrong, if he thinks that the team learned a lot and gained confidence that they can do the work in the future.

Mike brings in cake to celebrate the knowledge gained from the sprint. 'Sometimes sprints fail because a team tried to do too much,' Mike comments, 'so I still want to reward them because of how much they have learned from their attempt.'

Hardening sprints: Agile or not?

Some groups have three sprints per train and reserve the last sprint as a 'hardening sprint'. A hardening sprint is where you resolve all the bugs or issues hanging over from previous sprints before your train leaves.

Some Agile enthusiasts say you can't have a hardening sprint and really be Agile; otherwise, you would have got all your bugs and software fixes completed in the actual sprint in which they occurred.

Transitioning a company to Agile

Kelly Waters handled the transition of IPC Media to Agile. He explains how he did it:

First, we changed the structure. There was a classic functional structure, organised by role. Any requests for changes had to be coordinated across six different teams.

Change requests were coming in from all over the place and had to go through a central division serving many business units, all with their own requirements and priorities.

This structure might work for waterfall-based development, but not Agile. Our company is very dynamic with about 200 website releases per month.

If you think of a development spectrum with Chaos on one end with Formal development on the other, then Agile is somewhere in the middle. It's rigorous, but gives you a lightweight framework to function in.

We changed the company so we were set up in a way that was ready for Agile.

The first thing I did was align with the business and make our departments product focused. I kept the infrastructure central, but split people into divisional teams, aligned with our products. I then broke down each division into product teams, each with a portfolio of products.

Each product team has all the skills it needs to deliver requests from start to finish without reference to other teams. It's easy then to align priorities of the team with priorities of the business.

In addition, we moved people from around the building and sat product teams together. We even knocked down walls to make the ideal space for collaboration.

CHAPTER 4: BUSINESS PEOPLE AND DEVELOPERS WORK TOGETHER DAILY

Very few men are wise by their own counsel, or learned by their own teaching. For he that was only taught by himself had a fool for his master.

Ben Jonson

Breaking the Addiction to Process Step 4: Stop the mindset of *us* (the workers) versus *them* (the customers). In Agile, you work so closely with your customers that *us/them* becomes *we*.

This chapter describes how managers, developers and their customers can work together more cohesively. By abandoning the old 'master–slave' paradigm and really listening and learning from each other, the chances of your project succeeding substantially increase.

There is more conversation in Agile projects than in traditional ones. You don't just have one big meeting upfront to decide everything – then the engineers take it away and do it. Instead, there is a continuous conversation between customers and engineers over the course of the project in which requirements can change.

A continuous conversation

Through this conversation, engineers who are developing the products have a much better understanding of what the customer really wants because they are in frequent communication.

Kelly Waters comments:

It's important to go through this change because business alignment is critical. It enables close collaboration, clear ownership and prioritisation and forges strong human relationships, rather than just customer–supplier ones.

It makes a profound difference to work together more closely and meaningfully. More ownership and strong relationships means a greater commitment to delivery, quality and innovation.

People start to think about how they can improve *their* product, which makes a big difference.

Using the Agile methods of sprints, giving the stakeholder demos or prototypes at the end of sprints, and by following the Definition of Done that you agree at the start of the project, your customers can follow your team's progress more closely and it's more likely you'll deliver what they want when they want it.

A good way to converse about work

In early conversations between the stakeholders and engineers, you make high-level decisions about the project such as determining the epic and themes of the project.

An epic is the overall story for the project. An epic is too big to be estimated right away, so it's broken down into user stories that can be done in sprints. An example of an epic in daily life could be, 'As a host, I want to be able to give my guests barbecued food.' (User stories are written from a different perspective than traditional requirements.)

A theme is a set of stories – you can group them under a theme to make them easier to understand. As an example from daily life, if you were giving a BBQ (that's the epic), themes could be 'Invitations and Preparations', 'Food and Drink' and 'On the Day'.

Collaborative management

A project manager explains how collaboration works:

Agile teams shape software systems using a collaborative process, with executable software at its heart and documents marginalised to a peripheral role.

That's not to say documentation isn't vital, but that you shouldn't spend as much time upfront creating documents first, then trying to execute them later. The documents and software development should flow together and be updated at regular intervals.

Where does the product manager fit in?

Steve Borthwick comments:

Ideally, your product management person needs to be part of the daily stand-up. The downside of course is that code development is not an activity that is best done with constant interruption; a balance must be struck between communication and productivity. Ideally, conversations and discussions need to be batched up as much as possible and programmers need to be protected to some degree from being knocked 'out of the zone'.

Transparency and collaboration

Todd Thayer comments:

Transparency and collaboration is a key to success. My company created a Go-To-Market process for aligning the organisation to get the most out of launching products.

I think it would be a good idea if R&D departments did something similar. Chief Information Officers (CIOs) should be assigned to each major project; their job is to use the internal social networks and face-to-face interaction to vet the program and project plans. I'm not suggesting that R&D be run by a series of internal social responses, but having visibility into current plans would allow a company to minimise major mistakes during development. Having a point-of-contact between R&D and the rest of the company facilitates a level of transparency that will make our solutions more competitive.

Silos are for farmers

For a company to have a clear and unifying vision that can be executed swiftly, management, objectives and incentives must be aligned. No real cooperation can happen when teams are in their own little worlds and any engagement with another group can result in turf wars and unnecessary meetings to determine who is boss (for example, if a team's roadmap conflicts with another team's and meetings must be convened to decide whose roadmap will prevail).

Silos are a corporate evil and foster distrust and poor communication. A corporate common target, with groups working together to meet it, is the key to success.

Playful is the new serious

Collaboration with people you used to oppose (customers versus developers in the old mode) doesn't have to be a grim process. When you throw out the old ways of thinking about project management, you can also throw out the idea that it is a totally serious business too.

With global markets tightening and business stakes higher than ever, you'd think management theories would espouse

increased seriousness and stern sense of purpose. But no –
as a by-product of new ways of thinking about management
comes the idea that a sense of playfulness and fun increases
productivity.

If you aren't playing well, the game isn't as much fun. When that
happens, I tell myself just to go out and play as I did when I was
a kid.

Thomas J. Watson, founder of IBM

But it's not about employees enjoying their jobs more
because some of the tension and stress of making deadlines
has been lessened – it actually gives project managers vital
information about what functionality can actually be
achieved when a sense of play is injected into a team.

You can discover more about a person in an hour of play than in
a year of conversation.

Plato

You read about Planning Poker in Chapter 2. Agile
methodologies have also spawned other playful tools to
help with project management. One of them is Scrum Lego
City – a game that allows your team to simulate a real
scrum. You and your team try to build a city with all the
planning and arguing that entails. Here's an overview from
the game's website:

Find out how powerful scrum can be

Learning by doing, and failing. Do not underestimate any story ...
it may cost you a lot! The Scrum Lego City[4] brings you right to
the point: you will experience what it means to be Agile.

---

[4] Scrum Lego City by agile42 is licensed under a *Creative
Commons Attribution-Share Alike 3.0 Germany License*

The materials included in the game give you a clue to what you need to do to be Agile in your real workplace: this can help give you ideas on how to incorporate a sense of play in your group. Here's what the game contains:

- Lego with plans (possibly creative boxes where you can build many things with the same blocks);
- product vision: a document containing the vision to build the Lego city;
- requirements and user stories (cards): pre-compiled requirements and stories related to various building and elements of the city;
- Planning Poker cards;
- whiteboard or electrostatic sheets to write sprint outcome and velocity and make a whiteboard for the team;
- Post-its to write tasks;
- pen and whiteboard markers;
- unexpected (cards): some cards containing unexpected behaviour to steer from outside the game (you are ill or you leave the team); cards also contain suggestions on what people should do in particular situations.

Ways to keep everyone working together

Steve Borthwick uses these processes to help keep engineers and the customers working together effectively:

Daily stand-up meetings, short and sharp, driven by the developers – Vital so that managers can pre-empt issues and developers can communicate any issues, success, learning and progress. Also pretty important for QA, so that they get visibility of what's coming down the track and what might be easy or hard, and so on. No excuses for missing the stand-up, everyone is involved and speaks for an average of three to five minutes. If someone is working from home, then their stand-up has to be e-mailed into the team and read out by a colleague.

Code walkthroughs – Ideally, between a senior and a junior person, these have to be ego-less (this is hard). The purpose is manifold – for example, skills transfer, adoption of best practice, problem resolution, enforcement of consistent coding style and practice, optimisation.

Weekly backlog review meetings – Product management needs to review the backlog continually and triage it. Ideally, as we approach the start of a sprint, then the top *N* items on it represent our best bang for buck in terms of the things to work on. In practice, this is really hard to do in a small team.

Weekly architecture review meetings – Building the right system is more important than building the system right, but if you don't build it right then you've also failed (it just takes longer to find out). We use architecture reviews to help plan the content of sprints and to make sure that we stand the best chance of having software that scales and is as cheap as possible to own.

Weekly management review meetings – Management needs to be informed about progress (obviously); it helps to plan out sales engagements, set client expectations and also advises product management and development where the business priorities lie. It's hard to strike a balance between detail and overview; having a system that keeps track of metrics like burn-down and status really helps.

Monthly all-team member meetings – A software development team is not just about developers. Sometimes it's useful to hear things from the horse's mouth – for example, a sales person telling you which features the customers really like and which ones they don't, or an implementation consultant moaning about something that's hard to do, or congratulations on a problem solved and so on. It's not just developers who have good ideas either.

Monthly technical debates and team training – New technology and techniques are like food for programmers; it is important that best practice is communicated and also imparted. Discussions about the myriad ways of doing things, and debates on the best technology or design patters to use, are key to ensuring that people remain engaged and also feel like they are not stuck in a rut.

Getting business people to commit more time

Kelly Waters comments that one downside of Agile is that it's very time-consuming and demanding on business people who might not have been so involved before. He says:

I've found that people are very willing to engage but in some organisations this might be difficult to achieve. But I say this – if you can't get business people to commit to the project, is it really worthwhile?

CHAPTER 5: BUILD PROJECTS AROUND MOTIVATED INDIVIDUALS

Good men are the stars, the planets of the ages wherein they live, and illustrate the times.

Ben Jonson

Motivation is the art of getting people to do what you want them to do because they want to do it.

Dwight Eisenhower

> Breaking the Addiction to Process Step 5: Stop micro-managing people – select your team members carefully then trust them to do the right things.

Agile cuts down on top-heavy management through the principle of building teams of motivated people who choose their own work, so don't need to be actively managed all the time. They can drive progress themselves as they feel listened to and valued in the team, and so have the inner motivation to succeed. 'I recruit people who communicate well and are full of ideas,' explains one manager.

Steve Borthwick comments on this principle of Agile:

It is not something that is specific to software or Agile, but people need to be allowed to take risks and make mistakes.

It's far preferable to have someone on the team who solves their own problems and learns than someone who sits in their cube waiting to be told what to do next.

If people feel like they cannot take risks or experiment, then you end up with a very brittle and inefficient team. People also need to feel like the company is taking advantage of new ideas and better technology. The most common reason I hear in job interviews for people wanting to leave a company is that they feel the company is allowing them to fall behind their peers in terms of current knowledge of their art.

Engineers choose their own work

In the old mode of working, managers decided who on the team would do specific work items. Maybe the team member liked the work assigned, but more probably they didn't, and the manager had to 'explain' to them why they would like it.

In Agile, teams are more motivated to do the work because they choose it themselves. Managers can tell a team what work needs to be done, but the teams themselves decide how to handle the work load and get it finished and delivered.

Mike Rhodes says: 'Empowerment is the most important thing in an Agile team. If you trust people, they'll take more responsibility because they care about meeting the targets because *they* set them.'

How do you keep people motivated even when they feel stressed and overloaded? If they feel that they are really learning something and being challenged in a good way, the motivation will stay with them. But the most important thing is to make them the drivers of their own work. Let them decide the work to be done in a sprint and execute it. When problems come up, they will be more motivated to solve it themselves, rather than looking to a manager for solutions.

Giving up control

Some managers fear empowering team members because a more powerful team might take some action, or make a decision that the manager would not have made. But you can't over-control your teams. It is the responsibility of a manager to know what's going on, but not to micro-manage.

It's best if you can pick your own team and hire motivated workers who will inspire and enthuse other team members.

An Agile practitioner explains:

Picking your own team, instead of having a team foisted upon you from the engineering talent available, is a tricky situation.

In these scenarios, I would try to select at least one person that I wanted for the team, but if that's not possible, I would use at least one person on the existing team who has the ability to bring enthusiasm and energy to the group.

From this point, you can begin expanding the Agile methodologies. The mediocre workers will either look elsewhere for a more comfortable place, and those who have fallen into bad habits will feel renewed and want to participate. All this is provided that the company or higher management team is really committed to Agile in practice and not just talking a good game.

Management must be serious about Agile

Another problem can occur when the first team to become Agile upsets other more traditionally run teams in the company. That's when management must decide if it is playing at being Agile, or if it is serious about transforming the corporate culture to a new way of thinking.

If higher management does not take the new Agile teams seriously, the entire experiment can fail because the enthusiasm of the original Agile team will die.

IBM, one of the biggest Agile companies in the world, realises this danger. The company now recognises Agile teams for their accomplishments to keep them motivated and on track.

'We firmly believe, and our executives firmly believe, that the most successful organisations of tomorrow will be the ones [able] to adopt Agile principles,' one of their architects said at the SD West Conference 2008 in Santa Clara, California.

Too secretive for Agile

What about managers who are too secretive and hierarchical to go Agile? Can you shame them into going Agile by starting a mini-scrum team in your group and starting to live the life of transparency and openness in your work?

Anthony Lucas, an Agile coach at Nokia, thinks you can gradually transition a team whose members are initially sceptical of Agile methodologies by starting to have scrum teams anyway:

If part of a team tries Agile, and the others observe what is going on, and that it leads to more efficiency and communication, they will begin to join in a bit themselves. Once they see how the system works, they feel more relaxed and able to participate.

Lucas points out that managers don't have a role in scrums anyway, except to observe, so you can go ahead and try scrums and see how they work.

5: Build Projects Around Motivated Individuals

Kelly Waters thinks this gradual approach to Agile doesn't work. He says:

Change is a journey. People who are going through change go on a common journey. You have to take everyone on that journey with you.

Different people are at different stages at different times. At my company, I presented an introduction to Agile, what I saw as the problem, the need for change and how I thought we needed to address it.

I didn't only present to my teams. I presented to anyone and everyone. You cannot launch your initiative to adopt Agile in isolation and expect people to jump on board. It just won't happen. You have to lead the change, and take everyone with you.

CHAPTER 6: CONVEY INFORMATION VIA FACE-TO-FACE CONVERSATION

Talking and eloquence are not the same: to speak, and to speak well, are two things.

Ben Jonson

> Breaking the Addiction to Process Step 6: Stop hiding behind presentation slides and spreadsheets – get out and really communicate with your team.

How many times have you nodded off in a meeting? You are desperately trying to keep up with the slides being presented at the front of the room, but they are confusing with lurid colours and flying animation to jazz them up. All the jazzing-up does is kill any simplicity in the message, so you can't understand it at all.

Jargon Blitz

As if the slides weren't bad enough, what about the jargon-packed speech you have to listen to? You can barely understand any of it, yet it sounds so impressive – surely the speaker must know something that you don't? It all sounds good – but what exactly is he saying?

Ian Rowland labels this technique 'The Jargon Blitz'. He says, 'The use of arcane terms makes the presentation impossible to follow logically, and reinforces the idea that the person is an authority figure with secret knowledge.'

When the last slide set has been shown and the droning has ceased, you stagger back to your desk, unable to remember clearly what you just heard.

Afterwards, management congratulates itself for its fine communication with the team. They didn't even notice that they weren't listening to their employees at all, just telling them what's what. If that's communication, workers will take silence any day.

The Agile answer to death by PowerPoint®

Agile's answer to formalised meetings, with unending slide shows as the main communication tool, is the scrum.

A scrum is unlike any other team meeting you've ever attended. Imagine your manager not being able to say a word the whole time; in fact, having to stand and listen intently to everything the team says. Also, imagine being able to choose something you'd like to work on, rather than being told what to do from on high. Not only that, but imagine the show-offs who usually hog a meeting by talking about nothing while you sit silently suddenly being limited in the amount of time they can speak. Employee heaven or what?

One first-time scrum attendee commented on the wonder of it all:

It was so strange to be standing next to the boss, but she couldn't say a thing. She's usually outspoken and brusque, but in the Agile way of working, we have more power. We have a say in the tasks we want to do, and much more input into how the team is run. Anything that curtails the power of the bosses to ruin projects is fine by me.

A chicken and a pig

A chicken and pig Agile anecdote illuminates why bosses can't speak. Say that a chicken and pig are going to open a restaurant. The pig is going to contribute bacon, and the chicken will give eggs. The chicken is not committed to the project in the same way the pig is, so the chicken must be silent. 'Only pigs can talk in the scrum', Mike Rhodes explains, 'because if chickens (managers) talk, they might start micro-managing, and we want to avoid that.'

Also, if a manager directs a team to do this or that, then they have a pre-conceived idea of how the project is going to go and be completed, and that's not Agile. Agility comes from being flexible and responsive to the needs of the stakeholders and the marketplace. If you are flexible enough to bend to the changing needs of business, you will end up with a better product and a happier customer.

But scrum teams themselves shouldn't try to come up with finite solutions to issues raised in a scrum either because problems evolve too quickly and change too fast to be solved at a single stroke. It's important to let things evolve in Agile and not jump the gun for a solution just because it feels odd doing things in a new and different way.

Product owners and scrum masters

The scrum team is at the core of an Agile project. It consists of the scrum master, the product owner and the team. The team members must be engineers with the skills required to produce a piece of software that could be released to the customer by the end of a sprint.

Working in a scrum team demands a completely different mindset from traditional project meetings. In a scrum, there is no boss; the scrum master facilitates the meeting to make sure people stay on topic. The engineers are empowered to come up with solutions themselves. In fact, if your manager even tries to speak, he must be silenced (not permanently, but for the duration of the meeting).

Product owners and scrum masters are not the same thing, as they often have conflicting interests. The product owner wants to get features developed, and the scrum master wants to protect the team and keep obstacles out of their way.

Where does the scrum fit in the Agile world?

To refresh your memory from the overview earlier in the book, scrums belong with sprints. Remember that a sprint is a small period of time – for example, two weeks – needed for the team to come up with some working functionality that can be demonstrated or delivered to the customer. The team that does the work for a sprint is its scrum team.

After one sprint ends, another one begins based on lessons learned from the previous iteration. Learning lessons and continuously doing things better is the essence of agility.

The goal of the scrum

As with most Agile concepts, the goal of the scrum is transparency. A scrum promotes clear communication and the breaking down of obstacles that stand in the way of a team's progress.

Teams communicate every day using a few ground rules, so scrums don't become interminable and ineffective like big group meetings can be.

One engineer suggests:

Bring the core people (techies and management) from different teams responsible for a programme delivery into a single room; the rest of the team can be in different places. This core programme office team can coordinate with their respective teams and align the design and delivery. This is already practiced in Microsoft.

Mike Rhodes from Nokia says a good idea is to have a super scrum:

So all scrum teams know what each other is doing, it's a good idea to have super scrums. That's where you have all your scrum masters go to super-scrum meetings and spread resources.

What did you do yesterday? What will you do today?

Scrums are not status meetings. You don't reel off a list of stuff you've been doing for the past week and hope your manager doesn't notice any task inflation you've added. Scrums are to make progress in the project. The scrum master is there to help team members work effectively by reducing any impediments they are encountering.

The scrum master asks each team member in turn the following questions:

- What did you do yesterday?
- What will you do today?
- What is blocking you?

They might not have to ask these questions after the team gets used to the scrum rules. The ground rules of these daily scrum meetings are:

- Everyone stands up. No one gets to sit down or lean against a cabinet (people do try it at first though because they like to push the boundaries or hate to be team players – you can do something about unmotivated team members at a later date however).

- You can only talk about what happened in the last 24 hours. You tell the group what you've been working on and anything that is blocking your progress. (If you have been twiddling your thumbs for the past day, they will be able to tell that too.)

- Any veering off the subject or rambling will be quickly corrected by the scrum master who has been trained to handle these types of meetings.

- A prompt start is essential. People can't just drift in when they feel like it. In fact, the last person to join a scrum has a penalty of the team's choosing. Generally, the team's 'punishment' for the latecomer is that they have to go first at the next scrum, but some teams in America are more merciless, even making the delinquent team member sing a George Michael song, the video of which then goes on YouTube.

It's best to have your scrum meetings at a specific time that can't be changed, or else it can drift and your team starts skipping days. Discipline should be built into the scrum from the beginning.

Also, bring a baton to the meeting. Only the person holding the baton can speak – that keeps the meeting focused and sharp.

Jeff Gross, a Technical Executive and Software and Systems Information Architect in San Diego, says:

For engineers early in their careers, scrum is a great way to learn technical skills, technical job rotation and leadership (through self-organisation). For the more senior engineers, it can be a mixed bag, since previously recognition might have been for personal accomplishments (for example, being the 'hero'), experience (value independent of specific technology), and even the dreaded 'longevity'. The best senior engineers maintain an open mind and embrace many aspects of agility.

Importance of the whiteboard

The scrum team usually has a focal point for their gatherings, which should be a whiteboard. Just as a Victorian family would have gathered around the hearth in the evenings, the scrum team will gather around a board that has their backlog and sprint tasks written on it.

A scrum team writes their sprint tasks on Post-it notes on the left side of a whiteboard. Someone from the scrum team comes along, takes the task and puts their name on it and takes responsibility for it. This means anyone passing by the board can see the status of the project which helps transparency – the product owner or stakeholder can see how the project is going at any time.

The whiteboard will have columns such as:

- To Do
- Impeded
- Doing
- Done.

The scrum team will have Post-it notes in each of these columns. If an engineer can't do a task because of some obstacle, it goes in the Impeded column and stays in the product backlog. The scrum master talks with the team about the tasks on the whiteboard during the daily stand-ups. The scrum master tries to discover what is blocking a task being completed, so they can work to remove it.

Some groups have this information imaginatively displayed like a roadway or racetrack, so they can see their progress against the final goal at the end of the line.

About working around a whiteboard, one engineer suggests:

How about no more PowerPoint slides. Give everybody a tablet or virtual whiteboard to draw on, and make meetings interactive instead. How many times when you have a face-to-face meeting do you pick up a marker and start writing on a whiteboard?

I think we should also ban 'road mapping' practices that are often 90 per cent in PowerPoint. All that information could be in SharePoint and kept up-to-date and accessible to those who need it.

I really hate to see slides that mean there is no execution but just talk.

The location of teams

Ideally, teams should be situated in the same location, but that can difficult in our era of globalisation. In a perfect Agile world, you don't have juniors, outsourced teams or cultural constraints.

It's best if your team is local, so you can talk easily, have face-to-face time and use a whiteboard to write down all you're working on.

An Agile enthusiast at a large organisation comments:

We should put the people of a company back in focus. Help us build relationships with trust and a fighting spirit. The current state of my company is geographically spread clusters with virtual teams governed by global functions. Most meetings are with telcos; that means multi-tasking and time-slicing to the extreme. Line managers have dozens of direct reports.

It's a slow, but sure, death. This is not a way to make propositions that thrill our consumers.

A company gets into a good cadence (rhythm) of work when teams are located in the same place; if teams are not together, management must decide whether it can handle the costs of having the team travel to meet with each other once a quarter perhaps. Otherwise, communication is slower because of time zone differences and having to set up meetings to talk, since team members won't just run into each other in the hall of the office, for example.

A big company can have 200 scrum teams, so some strategy for communication should be in place, for example, a meeting of all scrum masters in a super-scrum.

The challenges of working in another time zone

Working in a geographically diversified team has its own set of challenges, like managing meetings, work distribution and dealing with cultural differences.

David Black from Nokia says:

You need to have face-to-face time to be Agile, but new video conferencing tools can help. A Halo meeting room, for example, makes you feel like meeting attendees are right there in the room with you.

Since the teams and sometimes the team members of a team are diversely spread, it is good practice to bring all of them in sync and rhythm at the beginning and at the end of the project. All the members of the scrum, therefore, meet at a common site and participate in the initial few scrum cycles.

Sharing Agile teams

Also when teams are spread out over the globe, there can be conflicts over how to divide up work. Kelly Waters says:

One of the challenges is how to share an Agile development team. You can't afford a whole, self-sufficient team for every product, as portfolios include products that sometimes report up to different areas.

The way we solved this problem at IPC Media is quite simple:

- Every product has an assigned product owner.

- Every product owner has their own product backlog for their product.

We decide how much of the team's time we want to dedicate to each product. For example, three products might be split 50/25/25 per cent, so we divide the sprint budget in those proportions.

Each product owner knows their particular sprint budget (in points). You get what you pay for. No more. No less. By sharing in this way, a team can be big enough to possess all the skills it needs, whilst still giving each product owner control of their priorities, without negotiating with other product owners.

CHAPTER 7: WORKING SOFTWARE IS THE PRIMARY MEASURE OF PROGRESS

Weigh the meaning and look not at the words.

Ben Jonson

Breaking the Addiction to Process Step 7: Stop working long hours to impress management – it's only the results that count.

This chapter discusses a new way of thinking about productivity – it's not how many hours you work, what your professional qualifications are or who you know – it's how often your team produces a working piece of software, no matter how small, for the customer.

Steve Borthwick explains:

This is important for the rest of the business to buy into. In most business fields, it's harder work or more hours that are the measures to watch; these are much easier to track. Ideally, you need to come up with some measures that correlate to the 'usefulness' of your product. In our case, we have such measures and they centre on the 'relevance' of the content we deliver; the tracking mechanisms are built into the product itself, so the measurement is fairly straightforward.

Measuring results

Don't listen to people, who tell you everything is great on the project, if they don't have evidence to back up the claim; that is, do they have a prototype or a piece of code that works without needing to be debugged?

The team and product owner should discuss acceptance tests during planning for each requirement, and agree on the Definition of Done before the start of each sprint.

Software code that is declared 'done' has passed the tests agreed by the team and the product owner, which means that it is potentially shippable to the customer.

An Agile Definition of Done can mean:

- Does the code to be delivered create value?
- Does the code meet the agreed quality criteria?

An example of Definition of Done

Rob Pardy at Nokia uses the following Definition of Done for his testing group:

The Definition of Done for project completion confirms that the development is complete (works, tested and error free) and is able to be handed back to maintenance on an ongoing basis, that is:

- Architecture is approved.
- Security has not been compromised.
- Configuration is approved.
- Test cases have been approved (work package and regression).
- Testing has been performed with results provided (work package and regression).
- No outstanding errors (handover might be agreed in specific cases).

Mike Rhodes says this type of Definition of Done is a change from the days of waterfall project management when you'd see the software code was checked in and it would be announced that the project was completed, but no one would say: Wait! Has this been tested? Does it actually run?

Mike adds:

You still have limited resources in software projects, so you can't do all you'd like. You still have to manage dependencies. And most of all, don't slip into cowboy coding because you think the Agile world is so flexible.

Not so many bottlenecks in Agile

Franz Andersson has been a system architect in both the new world of Agile and in the old mode of traditional project management. He says it is much easier to get software out to customers now.

In the old days, Franz did all the system requirements, design and architecture upfront without speaking to different stakeholders or customers on the project. He explains how difficult the way of working was then:

We gathered all our requirements and put them in a planning tool. The trouble started when we had to wait for someone in another group somewhere else in the world to make essential software changes before we could continue with our work. We were always waiting or trying to get permission to do some work that would affect another developer's tasks outside our team.

Now we don't have that problem anymore. All the people we need to do the work are in one scrum team, and we communicate frequently. And if we find we don't have the necessary team members to complete the goals of the sprint, we disband the sprint, communicate what's happened to the stakeholders, then reform in another sprint that tackles the problem in another way.

Franz explains an issue his team had when they did things in the traditional way:

There were two teams trying to accomplish the same goal, but we didn't know because we didn't communicate like we do now. We only found out about the duplication when the code was checked in and we saw the replication. That wouldn't happen now; we talk much more and have a greater awareness of what is happening in different groups within the company.

Ways to implement the new approach

As part of adopting a new approach, Steve Borthwick and his company Artesian Solutions put in place some new systems and made the use of others more formal. Steve comments, 'I could not imagine this approach without systems like this in place; I believe it would be too difficult.' Here are the systems Steve used:

- **A centralised software change control system and, more importantly, one that does branch and merge** – When there is a relatively short time between releases, significant bug fixes and 'spikes' around new features need to be done in separate branches and then merged back into the trunk. If you can't do this, then the change control process starts to inhibit the speed at which the releases (or sprints) can go. There is a 'drag-along' technical debt associated with allowing revisions to become too different that pulls you back into a less continuous mode if you let it.

- **A continuous build mechanism and rapid reporting of build breakages** – Since features are selected (size-wise) to fit within the scope of the sprint, it is important that developers can keep track of the current build and its status. If the build is unavailable for any reasonable length of time, it inhibits unit testing and integration testing, slowing the release down.

- **A build provisioning system**; that is, a mechanism where people can easily get hold of the latest build, primarily for testing purposes – Testers and developers need quick and easy access to the latest build. This is harder than it sounds when you have a few million lines of code, many projects and lots of data to keep in sync. If you delay them, or cause friction around provisioning, it can slow your release cycle down.

- **A consistent development environment** among all developers (no exceptions!) – Nothing worse than having to revert a feature because it only works in the latest whizz-bang version of a developer's environment; developers love to play with the latest stuff. The problem is that, unmanaged, this causes problems and delays, as differences crop up that need to be addressed (usually involving lots of stress).

- **An integrated unit testing mechanism** – Testing must be a fundamental part of development. Not only is this good practice anyway, unless software quality going into QA is good then releases are delayed; if the testing burden becomes too great, then the whole development/delivery process is slowed down. This is not only because testing takes longer, but also because re-work interrupts the progress of the next sprint over and above any planned allowance for it.

- **Integrated workflow/ticketing system** (integrated with the development environment) – Control is the great downside to Agile. Faster changes means more management; so, unless you are able to have dedicated resources and/or a good work management system in place to take the burden, then the management process itself can be a drag on the velocity of the team.

- **Integrated document management system** (integrated with ticket system and development environment) – Product managers and designers still need to write specifications and communicate design ideas; often this means documents and diagrams. These things need to be readily accessible and subject to proper change control. Any excuse given to programmers not to 'read the spec' is usually grabbed with both hands, leading to delay and re-work.

Small incremental releases increase revenue

Kelly Waters says:

At IPC Media, Agile has been transformational. It's transformed our reputation for delivery. It's transformed our business relationships. And it's definitely transformed our ability to drive business growth. Some of the benefits include:

- Revenue has increased, from delivering small incremental releases.

- Our speed-to-market is better than it was before.

- Quality of the product is improved significantly, thanks to the constant two-way feedback and testing from the start.

Obviously it's more flexible. Product owners are not committing to large projects and signing off detailed functional specs. They can give the team constant feedback as the product is being developed, and change direction as they see working software and can judge better from that what they really want.

We've also seen less risk and better visibility. And it's more fun. We don't spend months pouring over lengthy formal documents, with change committees and lots of bureaucracy. We spend our time collaborating to create the right product.

CHAPTER 8: MAINTAIN A CONSTANT PACE INDEFINITELY

To endure, and go calmly on!

Ben Jonson

Breaking the Addiction to Process Step 8: Stop being a perfectionist and burning out your team to deliver over-engineered software.

In traditional projects, a team has a finish line – the last date the software can be delivered to a customer. Time is not managed as well as it could be – perhaps the team is slow to get going, but the deadline is unmovable. As the finish line comes in sight, teams go into overdrive mode, driven to deliver a complete software application.

A related point is that only in Agile do you get the bad news quickly. In a conventional project, bad news comes slowly, fooling everyone into thinking there's much more time left than there really is. By the time you know you're in trouble, it's too late to do anything about it, which is when the long hours start and the functionality gets cut, or the product is simply delivered in an unfit state.

Building in contingency time is the traditional panacea, but it doesn't help very much – if you don't know something is wrong, you can't use the contingency to put it right. Unused contingencies mean the project can appear to be ahead of schedule, so there's a tendency for everyone to relax – that is, until the trouble arrives and everything has to proceed at breakneck speed.

Teams working by old-fashioned methods can think, for example, that working overtime increases productivity.

Projects don't have to be perfect

They also want the project to be perfect – to match the specifications that were set at the first of the project – even if it contains over-engineering or functionality that isn't really needed for the software to meet the customer's requirements – but got put in because it matched some geek's idea of elegance.

A project manager explains:

Features are specified by analysts who are not usually end-users. Typically, they will collect large volumes of customer requirements, not all of which are needed by all users – indeed it's doubtful whether anyone will need them all. When a project gets into time trouble, features will be cut based on what's most difficult to implement rather than what's most useful, resulting in a product with gross omissions, 'to be remedied in a later version'. An Agile-type approach can avoid this because it frequently gets feedback from the end-user, who will say what absolutely must be included and what can be omitted if it's too much trouble.

In the Agile world, projects and plans don't need to be perfect. They need to be just good enough to give the customer what they want, not what you think they need.

For example, if you are designing a touch screen for a phone, get the basics in there and working first before you over-egg the design and add features that the customer doesn't even know they want. Adding too many elegant or trendy additions can jeopardise delivery and basic working functionality.

And get rid of the idea that things have to be perfect and that driving others to perfectionist ideals is a good idea. In life and in software, things just have to be good enough.

Perfectionism and the resulting rigidity it brings is a project and career killer (as well as the fact that you never have any fun in life). Making mistakes is the only way we learn. The Agile methodology realises this and builds team retrospection into the project cycle.

Perfectionism: 'a crime against humanity'

Psychology Today has a few words about perfectionism to enlighten us:

You could say that perfectionism is a crime against humanity. Adaptability is the characteristic that enables the species to survive – and if there's one thing perfectionism does, it rigidifies behaviour.

Because perfectionism causes people to take fewer risks – if it's not going to turn out perfectly, they don't want to even try – they become constricted at a time when the world is requiring increasing flexibility and innovative thinking.

In a software project, being a perfectionist can kill off any chance of success. Spending a lot of time trying to get code to be perfect is a waste of time because software evolution moves so quickly – by the time you code something perfectly, the customer and the market could have moved on. The best plan is to get something coded quickly, tested then start the process all over again to give the product more value.

Managing time in Agile mode

Time can be managed much more effectively using Agile methodology. You don't have to have the entire project delivered in one burst; rather, you plan functionality in epics, made up of user experiences and experience enablers, so you can work at a less driven pace and are less likely to be totally burned out and ready to quit by the end of the project.

Mike Rhodes explains:

What you're basically doing is bagging what the stakeholder wants and delivering it. In the old ways, if you do too much architectural work too soon, you do too much horizontal development and can get to the end of the project without anything to show the customer.

If you engineer product functionality in increments and test and show stakeholders, you can correct mistakes in your own perception of what the customer wants, and the customer can see what is really achievable – this helps foster communication and leads to project success.

Planning epics

A rough guide to planning elements for epics follows:

- **Money** – How much will you need for development tools, prototypes, software/hardware and people?
- **Effort** – How many months will you need for how many people to work as a team?
- **Time** – How many development trains will you require for an epic that lasts about a year?
- **Skills** – What kind of skills do you need to develop your product? What competencies do you need your engineers to possess?

Shorten the time between planning and delivery

Agile shortens the time span between planning and delivery, so teams can pace themselves better.

For example, by following the practice of continuously integrating code into the baseline product, instead of waiting until the end of a project cycle, no nasty surprises await a team. A team's results can be relied on because code is released continually and integrated.

Automate where possible

Another way to shorten the time span between planning and delivery is by automating as much as you can. For example, running an automatic test for a piece of functionality speeds the process more than having to turn the code over to a tester who takes it off to test.

Reusing existing documentation and UI design where possible helps automate too. If documents are written in modular components so certain sections can be repurposed, that saves time and effort.

Keep your goals visible

Instead of saying something like 'we need to deliver a housing benefits system to the government' – a big and rather nebulous goal – you break it down into working pieces of deliverable software; for example, 'we need to deliver software that will calculate a claimant's housing tax for one time period' instead.

Analysis paralysis

Steve Borthwick comments:

Software development is somewhat of a momentum game. Being a cerebral activity in the main, it is easy to fall into a state known as 'analysis paralysis', where people dither and hesitate endlessly analysing something for fear of making the wrong decision.

A sense of urgency around everything that is done is key if the goal of frequent releases is to be realised; sometimes it is better to make an inferior decision and move on rather than get stuck.

CHAPTER 9: GIVE CONTINUOUS ATTENTION TO TECHNICAL EXCELLENCE

He knows not his own strength that hath not met adversity.

Ben Jonson

Breaking the Addiction to Process Step 9: Stop taking so long to acknowledge mistakes – use the 'Fail Fast' principle to identify problems quicker.

Agile methodology speeds up the traditional project cycle. Scrum teams work in short iterative cycles with continual testing and code integration. Because code integration occurs at frequent intervals, there is less chance that a big code integration at the end of a long cycle will result in broken functionality and the ultimate failure of a project.

Use the 'Fail Fast' principle in your projects, then you can see what's wrong and needs re-planning, rather than waiting for a whole project to be completed. (A Fail Fast system is designed to report failures quickly and halt. In an IT company, for example, if a serious error occurs, the build can be completely stopped and the code blocked.) With Agile sprints, you aim to have a demo or prototype for the stakeholder regularly, so you'll know faster what isn't working. You can recover more quickly from mistakes because the cycle between planning and delivery is shorter.

User stories in Agile (requirements in traditional project terminology) must be testable. You don't have to know what the test will be in detail early on, but you must determine if it can be tested. If it can't be tested, break it down further into smaller functional units until it is testable.

When it becomes clear that your team can't do a user story within a sprint, declare that the sprint has failed and form another one quickly after re-planning.

Also, when it becomes clear that a feature can't be implemented with an epic, you should recognise the failure as fast as possible and remove it from the epic, so it's not cluttering up your product backlog.

Test-driven development

Agile development work is done in a test-driven environment; that is, any development work done must be tested continuously for quality and excellence. Some companies have monitors displaying integration results, so managers or any interested parties walking past can see if software code put into the master code line has compiled successfully or not.

A red icon next to the compiled code means there are errors; a green light means no errors have been found.

'With the status of my work displayed so prominently,' one engineer confesses, 'it motivates me to work fast to get problems sorted out.'

Automated testing

One of the keys to finding out what isn't working in a project quickly is using automated testing. Automation is essential for agility, otherwise you can't find problems fast enough.

Test cases should be developed in parallel with development in a sprint, so you can quickly test the resulting functionality. Manual testing is too slow, and your project is bogged down while engineers wait for the results. You can't fix problems quickly if it takes forever to test the code.

Steve Borthwick makes this point:

An integrated unit testing mechanism is very important in your project. Testing must be a fundamental part of development. Not only is this good practice anyway, unless software quality going into QA is good then releases are delayed. If the testing burden becomes too great, then the whole development/delivery process is slowed down. This is not only because testing takes longer, but also because re-work interrupts the progress of the next sprint over and above any planned allowance for it.

There might still be last-minute panic

'When end-users get involved in the final stages of testing, light bulbs go on, and they often have an "aha" moment – unfortunately, that is often too late' (Frank R. Parth, director of Project Auditors, a project management consultancy).

Even teams using sprints to do code in can still slip up and leave making demos and test cases until the end, but experience helps this situation improve. The collaborative work mode of Agile means engineers don't think of other people's tasks as separate entities – for example, 'It's not my job to test that' is less likely to be heard. Because teams self-organise and don't specialise as much, there's more collective responsibility for the overall results.

In Agile, managers can't ride teams hard at the last like a factory foreman might have done in the 1950s. There is a constant attention to detail because of the short sprints of work.

Ideally, some slack time has been built into the schedule also. Slack time gives the team an opportunity to handle issues that have occurred or correct errors.

Steve Borthwick's company has developed a continuous build mechanism and rapid reporting of build breakages. He explains:

Since features are selected (size-wise) to fit within the scope of the sprint, it is important that developers can keep track of the current build and its status. If the build is unavailable for any reasonable length of time, it inhibits unit testing and integration testing, slowing the release down.

Other areas need continuous attention, too

Documentation, testing and UI design are not separate groups or issues in the Agile world – you build those requirements into the sprint also, so it all gets done in a timely way.

Agile documentation

Old-fashioned documentation used to mean producing monolithic books of documentation that were so big they could be used for doorstops. It was hard to find information in them – they were too unwieldy.

Now we have modular components of documentation – for example, instead of 2,000 pages of text you can have a thousand topics that are able to be re-used as online help or PDF files. Not only does that cut down on unnecessary effort by writers, it makes the information easier to find for the consumer.

In addition, dynamic publishing tools offer customer-focused documents on demand (sending a PDF file to a customer instead of printing a user guide, for example).

A technical writer explains:

Documentation is not traditionally Agile because it is usually written only once in the project cycle or release and after all the software coding is finished. To be Agile, it should be written alongside the coding and made part of the sprint, along with UI work. Documentation should be alive and changing as requirements change, not something that is issued once a year on printed paper.

Also, instead of having a team of documentation people who don't sit near the developers or are not even in the same department, embed a writer in a scrum team, so they always know what's going on in the team.

As a rule of thumb, the best plan is to have one writer per scrum team, but the reality is usually there's more like one writer per three scrum teams. But that's still an improvement on the old set-up where a writer is not even part of the daily life of developers.

David Black, a senior documentation manager at Nokia, says to deliver documentation to small chunked deadlines: 'If software is developed that way, it must be documented that way so you can be sure of tracking the software changes'.

Agile UI design

A UI designer argues that her company needs to go Agile for these reasons:

9: Give Continuous Attention to Technical Excellence

Our core products and services should be designed and developed in one place because virtual teams deliver virtual experiences.

Every day I need to coordinate myself with people in Berlin, London, Boston, Bangalore and New York. All this effort kills quality, time to market, assets and resources.

The quality of our UI is very poor because we design to present over a conference call and not for actual use. We never cover details because they cannot be explained over a one-hour teleconference.

Many times the threshold between failure and success is razor thin, but we are always too far away and we take uninformed decisions.

We are not able to deliver results because of the way we work and no one is accountable; therefore, all our roadmaps and strategies become academic dissertations.

In essence, continuous testing and integration of code and doing documentation and UI activities in parallel with development speeds up the project cycle, so you can deliver something to the customer faster than ever before.

CHAPTER 10: SIMPLIFY – MAXIMISE THE AMOUNT OF WORK NOT DONE

Many might go to heaven with half the labour they go to hell.

Ben Jonson

Breaking the Addiction to Process Step 10: Stop mandating the deadlines – instead, ask the people in the trenches doing the real work how much they can do. In Agile terms, you ask the people making the pizzas how many pizzas they can make.

This chapter explains how Agile reduces the workload of an old-fashioned project that is burdened by too many meetings, slide presentations and dictates from authoritarian management by minimising the work needed to be done. Also, you need to avoid Parkinson's Law:

Work expands so as to fill the time available for its completion.

Observations of the British Civil Service in the 1950s showed that their numbers increased, even as their duties decreased with the decline of the British Empire. This was explained by John Murray in an essay in 1958. He wrote that the growth occurred because of two reasons:

- An official wants to multiply subordinates, not rivals.
- Officials make work for each other.

So, even if the workload is decreasing, people can make work for each other and find they need to hire more people to push paper around. We can see this happening in modern companies today, as groups busily prepare slides to show other workers and each other. The slides that one group engenders becomes part of a slide set for another group that then shows it to another department and so on.

How many times have you heard, 'Do some slides for this' to be sent to management instead of sending a simple e-mail or calling someone on the phone?

Agile methodology tries to cut down on the slides and even e-mail. Many groups put their information up on SharePoint®, so the information can't be lost in someone's inbox or left to die at the bottom of a long e-mail thread.

Minimal engineering

Minimal engineering is about moving from 'concept to cash' as quickly as possible with the least effort expended. As Taiichi Ohno pointed out when he was working on Lean Manufacturing for Toyota:

All we are doing is looking at the time line, from the moment the customer gives us an order to the point when we collect the cash. And we are reducing the time line by reducing the non-value-adding wastes.

How do you reduce the waste of time and effort? Here are some ideas:

Avoid software bloat

In the old days, software programs had to be precise and lean because computer memory was limited and to buy more space cost a lot of money. Software had to be efficient to run property. But as computer memory has expanded and become cheaper, software has become bigger and less efficient.

'Software bloat' is the term applied to software that boasts so many features that it's a resource full of useless functionality. As David Black at Nokia points out, the 80/20 rule applies – 80 percent of users only make use of 20 percent of the software written in an application – the rest of the code and effort is a waste. To be Agile, software is engineered to be modular and easy to re-use.

'The easiest of all wastes, and the hardest to correct, is this waste of time because it does not litter the floor like wasted material,' Henry Ford wrote in his 1926 book, *Today and Tomorrow.*

Remove activity that adds no value

Craig Borysowich, a technology tactician, says:

When looking at activities in a process, we must determine if the activity is effective and efficient. We must also determine if the activity can be improved to provide a better product or service for the customer.

If the activity could be removed from the process, with no effect on the end-product or service, it is an NVA (non-value-add) activity. NVA activities, also referred to as waste activities, often indicate deficiencies in the process design.

If you think of how much code in a project is written but never used, then why write it in the first place? That's how you maximise the work not done.

Engineers want their software to be elegant, so they might have a tendency to fuss over their work and want to add nice touches – but the stakeholders don't need this. They want the functionality they asked for, and don't care that somewhere some developer added some additional cool flourish.

Also, in companies run in traditional hierarchical ways, communication can be poor. Too often, one group in a company is working on the same thing as another, but they just don't know it. Reducing duplication of effort is an important way to maximise the amount of work not done.

Remember the concept of just-in-time manufacturing? Then think of this as *just-do-enough* engineering – it works on the same sort of Lean principle.

Parallel working

Parallel working speeds up your project's progress. For example, in a linear working process for documentation, writers can't write a document until the software is finished, and the document can't be reviewed until it is a completed document, so people end up waiting and wasting time.

But if you work in parallel in small teams, rather than one big team working on something and waiting for someone else to finish some other process, you save time and money.

Parallel working means less waste because people are working at a steady pace, not sitting around waiting. The goal is to keep all resources occupied at the same level of working.

Pair programming

Another way to reduce the number of specialists in your team is by pair programming – this is the concept of having two people working on one piece of code. Having two minds on a problem is better than one, and also problems can be discovered faster using this technique.

Get feedback as soon as possible

Get feedback as soon as possible to avoid wasting time and money (minimising the amount of reworking to be done).

Traditional projects had too much waiting built in – waiting for another group to get something done or for a manager to make a decision. You would send some code off to be put in a queue for testing, or to be integrated with something else and then returned with comments or problems

If you test in parallel with development in a shorter cycle, you get fewer errors, you waste less time and speed up the delivery of software and development

You are also learning continuously – maximising value, as well as doing a better job faster because you are learning.

Reduce bureaucracy

Chuck Wergrzyn from Nokia comments:

The idea with Agile programming isn't about having scrum meetings all the time, but about communication (and by extension collaboration). It's difficult writing a program without complete information, and it is just as difficult to build a system without it.

Stop worrying about meetings (meetings and more meetings), and just make sure there is complete communication between programmers (and managers). You'll soon have Agile development.

Make them pay for it

Kelly Waters has developed a sure-fire method of reducing his team's workload: he makes groups fund the functionality they request. He says:

Agile isn't just a way of working – it changes the way you interact with other areas of the business. Therefore, our business alignment didn't stop at the structure. We also aligned the money.

We aligned the money we recharge to the business units. If people are allowed free money, that is, they don't pay for the resources they consume, then there are no limits.

If you could have anything, for no cost, what would you ask for? Everything! It's only natural, but this simply doesn't work. Aligning teams with business units means we are also able to negotiate this once a year.

This is how we fund business-as-usual. In addition, projects are funded like this: if it's not important enough to prioritise or pay for, then it's not important enough to shout about.

Now we can have grown-up conversations about priorities.

'Who shouts the loudest' is no longer the system for getting things done.

CHAPTER 11: TEAMS SELF-ORGANISE

How near to good is what is fair!

Ben Jonson

> Breaking the Addiction to Process Step 11: Stop telling people what to do like it's 1959 – teams know better than a single manager what needs to be done.

In the old days, to improve productivity and quality, managers thought it was important to formalise the activities and tasks of the development process. In this kind of methodology people have to adapt to the process.

Agile methodology, however, has put people back at the centre of the development activities. In this kind of methodology 'people trump process', and processes have to be adapted to the needs of the workers.

But even Henry Gantt saw that was wrong in the early 20th century. He said:

Whatever we do must be in accord with human nature. We cannot drive people; we must direct their development ... the general policy of the past has been to drive; but the era of force must give way to the era of knowledge, and the policy of the future will be to teach and lead, to the advantage of all concerned.

(Even in the 21st century there are managers who still haven't realised this. Mike Rhodes comments: 'Some managers spend more time with their Gantt chart than with their people.')

The office is a social environment

In addition, the office is a social environment, so a big salary is not the whole story. Employees want to be recognised for their contributions, feel their job is safe and also feel that they are part of a good group of people working on an interesting product.

You can see how morale nosedives at companies in trouble. People want to feel like they are part of a successful company that is making things customers really want and value.

Also, workers like to have a friendly working relationship with their management. When employees feel valued and listened to, they respond by being loyal to the company and don't change their jobs as quickly.

All companies talk about empowering employees, but few do. Successful managers know that empowerment is crucial to getting good results, realising that their teams know far more about what's required than they do.

Companies need charisma

Arrogant companies that dictate to their employees leak dissatisfaction from every pore. (Have you read anonymous postings from disgruntled employees on Internet blogs?) When a company has humility and tries to put its people first, it displays corporate charisma and that can influence public perception and positive consumer decisions.

Lack of openness is another problem. Traditional management hates transparency because it threatens their control. They don't want employees to know what's going on behind the scenes. But transparency works both ways.

Management should also get transparency from engineers, so they have a better idea of the state of the project.

As Seymour Cray commented: 'The trouble with programmers is that you can never tell what a programmer is doing until it's too late.'

Don't manage like it's 1959

Over-directing people isn't good because how does a manager know better than an actual worker what should be done? Managers might think they know best because they worked on a bunch of specifications and requirements early on in the project, but that was a long time ago and things change.

In Agile, because there is no authoritarian leader in charge, teams organise themselves. When teams divide work up among themselves, risk is reduced (if a team depends on a strong authoritarian leader, for example, what happens if they get run over by a truck or leave the company?) and a supportive framework of working together is in place for the duration of the project.

Teams self-organise and decide what to work on themselves, rather than waiting to be told what to do by a manager who might not even understand the intricacies of the work involved. This speeds up the entire process. Decentralising control on a project means groups can deliver software faster without as many bottlenecks as before in traditional projects.

The transition from a 'command and control' corporate culture to one of self-organisation is not easy. It's even being debated as to whether there will, in future, even be someone on a team referred to as the 'project manager'.

How this would work for a team is in the example of a tester who complained that, 'I don't feel like a part of the team.' A team would have initially looked to the line manager to solve it, but of course it's a team problem now. Once they realised they owned the problem themselves, they came up with a solution (they moved the tester's desk to be in their group and included the tester in all future team discussions) and sorted it out.

Simplify decision making

An engineer at a Fortune 500 company says:

I believe if companies simplify their governance model they can achieve higher productivity. When I first joined my company, our culture was to have decisions made as low in the organisation as possible, so we were flexible and agile towards market changes.

Since those days, we have moved to become more bureaucratic. Decisions are made in leadership meetings, even though they could be done nearer to the action. Empowering people is a key to success. You have to take responsibility and ownership for whatever you are doing.

Losing clear ownership of projects means a loss of responsibility. If no one is sure who is responsible, then no one is accountable, and no one can make a final decision. When failure occurs in this scenario, blame and finger pointing afterwards is inevitable.

Such a scenario occurred recently in a big international company:

What should we do about this problem with the code?

I don't know. We can't make any decisions until the manager is back from his meetings with the bigwigs at headquarters.

Is he online? I can send him an e-mail.

No, he's not online. Don't you remember? He's in a team-building event with other managers. They are learning to work as a team by cooking a big meal together at a posh hotel.

Huh?

It's like one of those shouting-chef TV shows. The team has to prepare a big meal under deadlines and delegate tasks to each other under pressure. Then they learn to work together.

But this company has reorganisations every six months. What's the point?

I don't know, but they have the budget to do it, so I guess they are going to spend the money.

But what about our deadlines? Can we go ahead with the programming?

No, he has to be here to make the big decisions. You know how angry he gets if he's not consulted for every little thing.

But the customer wants to see this code working by next week.

(Shrugs shoulders.) *I'm not getting the boss mad at me. My job review is coming up.*

OK, I'll put it on the back burner. (Then nothing happens for weeks.)

With Agile, scenarios like this are less likely to happen. Teams drive their own work, and the manager has a more minimal role.

People get tired of war metaphors

Working in Agile mode also brings blessed relief for teams who are forever being told by their management that they are in a 'battle'. It's going to be tough and brutal, managers will explain, as if they are talking to actual troops about to face death, but if we work hard and stay focused we can do it. It gets tiring for employees to always be at war or in battles year after year – they will get post-traumatic stress disorder from the constant fighting, quit or just ignore the dire forecast.

We need to move on from the war and violence metaphors. Is this really the best way to inspire effective software development?

Self-directed teams

Because Agile means building smaller batches of code and that the team can direct itself with only minimal management, teams have higher productivity and delivery of code. This leads to greater satisfaction for workers and faster turnaround to the customer who is satisfied with the commitment and hard work of the company.

A tester explains:

The principle to self-organise is important. In our organisation, we ran into a situation that developers were fixing bugs at a very fast pace, and each sprint had more and more fixed errors waiting to be tested and verified by quality assurance.

Our testing backlog started growing, and I got nervous thinking that we'd never be able to keep up. Then one day the scrum master realised the situation and implemented a 'whole-team' approach. The developers got involved in clearing up the increasing testing backlog items. Then we saw the backlog diminishing. It is such a relief that we could put Agile principles to work in such a helpful way.

Changing the monolith

Changing a big monolithic organisation means moving decision making to lower levels in the organisation where the work is actually being done. An important step is listening to the opinions of your software team when creating roadmaps. (But, remember in Agile, roadmaps are just good enough to get you going; they aren't written in stone like in traditional projects.)

This means a company can reduce unnecessary managerial roles, reduce duplication and overlap of roles and simplify working procedures.

For example, in a sprint you might do one half of a user story – the team decides what it can get finished in two weeks. The goal is that all the managers get out of the way and let the team work and figure out what to do about problems themselves. But, if there are no micro-managers involved, there's also no excuse if the work isn't done because teams organise and direct themselves.

People talk about empowering their teams, but not much happens in reality with traditional methodologies. However, if you create an environment where each team member feels they can make a contribution or a difference to the outcome, the true power of a worker is unleashed. Creativity and innovative thinking comes when you feel free, not constrained by last century's thinking on project management.

This approach keeps quality high. You set the team up and let them run. Managers, however, must also resist the urge to go and tweak a requirement or alter a story.

Gore-Tex: an example of an Agile company

Gore-Tex is a good example of an Agile company. They got rid of the management hierarchy, so that anyone working for them can go directly to anyone else within the organisation for help. That's an amazing idea, especially if you think about some traditional companies where hierarchy is still the order of the day, and you can't approach anyone senior without first talking to one of their subordinates.

Even worse is the company where you don't even talk to the subordinate. If there's something outside your area, you have to refer it to your manager, who will talk to the other person's manager, or push it up the chain of command to the point in the hierarchy where managerial lines converge.

Another principle of Gore-Tex is that all the employees are owners of the company, so anything they do or don't do will impact the bottom line of their own pay packet.

The company studied Abraham Maslow and his views on how people react when they're not feeling safe and secure. A spokesman says, 'These philosophies set the foundation for our company's values. He knew that if you can't engage your associates, if they don't feel they can make a difference ... you won't get innovation.'

What a man can be, he must be

Consider Abraham Maslow's Hierarchy of Needs[5] for evidence of what makes a good workplace, and of how a company can change its culture to improve its bottom line.

In Maslow's Hierarchy, a person has the following needs in descending order (this list is tailored for the business world):

---

[5] Read his book *Motivation and Personality* (1954) for more information.

- **Self-actualisation** – You need to feel that you are reaching a potential from within yourself, whether it's inventing something or being a good leader.
- **Esteem** – You want respect, or at least to feel you are accepted for who you are, and that you don't have to pretend to fit in.
- **Love and belonging** – You want to feel part of something bigger. You want to feel that you belong in your group.
- **Safety needs** – You want to feel safe in your job.
- **Physiological needs** – You need your basic needs met – food, air, water and a decent place to do your job.

Maslow's theories give a powerful impetus to methodologies, such as Agile, because they verify that the approach works on a basic human level, that it's not just another silly management theory that will fade in time. Agile methodology answers our basic human needs of empowerment, recognition and belonging.

Because these theories apply to all humans, no matter which culture they were born in, it is a powerful tool for running projects or companies in a global marketplace. The need to feel you belong somewhere, that you make a difference, for example, is as true for a Chinese as for an American worker.

Working together requires a different kind of leadership

John Shook says:

There are three kinds of leaders. Those that tell you what to do. Those that allow you to do what you want. And Lean leaders that come down to the work and help you figure it out.

Mike Rhodes warns:

Don't throw away all your project management skills just because you've gone Agile. People can hijack the Agile manifesto and say they don't want to plan anything, but that's not the way it works. You don't want to get rid of all documentation or contracts or planning. It was too rigid in the old days, but that doesn't mean that Agile is anarchy. We still need leaders, but managers have to take a step back. They shouldn't rush in to handle everything anymore.

Ntissar El Allali makes this point about leadership:

Every project needs a leader. Agile methodologies free the project manager from the drudgery of being a taskmaster, thereby enabling the project manager to focus on being a leader. Agile project management places a higher premium on leadership skills than ever before.

Leading from the back

Kelly Waters agrees:

Agile teams need managers, too. Self-organisation is not boundary-less. Managers provide direction and guidance, and manage individual performance. They keep the team focused on objectives and help to solve problems. They support their teams, to help them be the very best that they can be.

In Agile, it's more like the manager reports to the team and not the other way around. I call it 'leading from the back'.

And finally, remember the words of Dwight D. Eisenhower:

You do not lead by hitting people over the head – that's assault, not leadership.

CHAPTER 12: TEAMS HOLD RETROSPECTIVES AND TUNE THEIR BEHAVIOURS

Success produces confidence; confidence relaxes industry, and negligence ruins the reputation which accuracy had raised.

Ben Jonson

Breaking the Addiction to Process Step 12: Don't move into the future without taking time to learn from your past mistakes.

Do you generally finish a project with great relief and move on quickly to the next thing without trying to learn from your mistakes? No one likes dwelling over errors they've made or bad judgement calls; but don't you want to learn something from it, so you won't repeat the same mistakes again?

Remember the axiom: 'If you're not making mistakes, you're not trying hard enough.'

It can be hard on the ego to review a situation where you have clearly screwed up, but Agile makes it easier to handle because you review your actions and accomplishments after every sprint (approximately after every two weeks).

That's the beauty of Agile. You're constantly correcting yourself.

We go off course all the time, in life and in work, so the faster we can get back on track, the better. In this way, Agile can help you even when you're not at work.

Sprint retrospectives

In Agile, you and your team have a retrospective at the end of each sprint. Because you are getting continual feedback through ongoing testing and integration work, you avoid wasting time and money because of the frequent periods of reflection.

Kelly Waters says:

With Agile development, these retrospectives enable the team to make small improvements regularly, and tackle changes in manageable, bite-sized pieces that can be actioned immediately.

Identifying and eliminating waste should not be a rare event conducted by process re-engineering consultants every few years. It should be a regular process, built into regular iterations, determined as much as possible by the team, and tackled in small, timely steps.

Making improvements little-but-often in this way creates a culture of continuous improvement – a learning environment – which, for some organisations, could potentially give you the edge over competitors.

So, if you're not doing it already, I urge you to hold regular retrospectives. This is one Agile development practice I can heartily recommend. Try to foster lively, but healthy, debate, critical, but constructive, feedback, and try to drive out meaningful and actionable improvements that actually help you to frequently identify and, more importantly, eliminate waste.

Working to the same heartbeat

Mike Rhodes says:

A guy said to me, 'This Agile stuff is stupid. What we really need is to get back to the basics of management – let's get rid of everything and just have a prioritised list of things we need to do and go down the list doing it,' and I said: 'But that's Agile.'

12: Teams Hold Retrospectives and Tune Their Behaviours

Working in the cadences (or rhythm) of Agile eases the work overflow and stress of teams, and, when an organisation works to the same principles and cadence, the entire company is working to the same heartbeat.

Status quo bias

It goes against human nature to change and innovate; that's why adopting Agile practices is not easy. We all have a status quo bias that means we resist change and prefer things to remain the same, unless there is some compelling reason that makes us want to change.

S.E. Smith writes in the blog Wise Geek: 'By being aware of the role that the status quo bias plays in their own lives, people can take steps to reduce the influence of this bias on their decision making … While the status quo bias can provide a certain amount of self-protection by encouraging people to make safer choices, it can also become crippling, by preventing someone from making more adventurous choices. Like other cognitive biases, this bias can be so subtle that people aren't aware of it, making it hard to break out of set patterns.'

Change isn't easy

Once we become aware of the limitations of conventional project management and the fact that we have to change our mind set to adapt to the new conditions, it's still very hard to do it.

Karen Blakeley, author of *Leadership Blind Spots and What to Do About Them*, points out:

There is no point reading about the practices, unless we are prepared to face the fact that implementing them will not be easy. More than anything, it will involve personal discipline. We have been told for too long that we have to instil leadership in organisations, inspire innovation and creativity, empower people, trust them, encourage teamwork, build a learning organisation ... but it doesn't happen. And it doesn't happen because of old learning (self-defeating beliefs and attitudes) and a fear of completing the learning cycle – that is, take action based on what we know is right. We rationalise this lack of learning and leadership by telling ourselves:

- We tried it before and it didn't work.
- There is too much to do already.
- It's too risky to challenge the status quo.
- There's too much at stake – I have a career to protect.
- I'm not a leader.
- This organisation will never change.
- I'm too busy.

... We can no longer rationalise our collusion with outdated organisational cultures by telling ourselves that taking action will be too difficult and will not help us achieve our goals.

Kelly Waters concludes:

It's true, I admit it. I think Agile development is brilliant. But let me tell you what Agile is not:

- Agile is not easy.
- Agile is not a silver bullet.

Successfully implementing Agile takes commitment, courage, leadership and tenacity.

To summarise, going Agile takes courage – the courage to change your way of thinking, the courage to respond quickly to change, and the courage to plan without Gantt charts.

12: Teams Hold Retrospectives and Tune Their Behaviours

Henry Ford said:

We do not make changes for the sake of making them, but we never fail to make a change once it is demonstrated that the new way is better than the old way. We hold it our duty to permit nothing to stand in the way of progress.

Go get 'em, Tiger

A good example of this sort of courage is Liza Cirlot Looser, the owner of The Cirlot Agency, a multi-million dollar corporate communications firm in Jackson, Mississippi.

Liza decided to strike out on her own in advertising. When she approached the owner of the agency she had worked for to impart her plans, he laughed and said, 'You'll never make it in this business'.

Undeterred, Liza went to the bank and, with a tiny $78 tax-return cheque in her hand, opened an account for her brand-new business. When the teller realised what Liza was doing, she smiled warmly and said: 'Go get 'em, Tiger!'

It's good advice for all of us.

ITG RESOURCES

IT Governance Ltd. sources, creates and delivers products and services to meet the real-world, evolving IT governance needs of today's organisations, directors, managers and practitioners. The ITG website (*www.itgovernance.co.uk*) is the international one-stop-shop for corporate and IT governance information, advice, guidance, books, tools, training and consultancy.

http://www.itgovernance.co.uk/project_governance.aspx is the information page on our website for project governance and Agile resources.

Other Websites

Books and tools published by IT Governance Publishing (ITGP) are available from all business booksellers and are also immediately available from the following websites:

www.itgovernance.co.uk/catalog/355 provides information and online purchasing facilities for every currently available book published by ITGP.

http://www.itgovernance.eu is our euro-denominated website which ships from Benelux and has a growing range of books in European languages other than English.

www.itgovernanceusa.com is a $US-based website that delivers the full range of IT Governance products to North America, and ships from within the continental US.

www.itgovernanceasia.com provides a selected range of ITGP products specifically for customers in South Asia.

www.27001.com is the IT Governance Ltd. website that deals specifically with information security management, and ships from within the continental US.

Pocket Guides

For full details of the entire range of pocket guides, simply follow the links at *www.itgovernance.co.uk/publishing.aspx*.

Toolkits

ITG's unique range of toolkits includes the IT Governance Framework Toolkit, which contains all the tools and guidance that you will need in order to develop and implement an appropriate IT governance framework for your organisation. Full details can be found at *www.itgovernance.co.uk/products/519*.

For a free paper on how to use the proprietary Calder-Moir IT Governance Framework, and for a free trial version of the toolkit, see *www.itgovernance.co.uk/calder_moir.aspx*.

There is also a wide range of toolkits to simplify implementation of management systems, such as an ISO/IEC 27001 ISMS or a BS25999 BCMS, and these can all be viewed and purchased online at: *http://www.itgovernance.co.uk/catalog/1*.

Best Practice Reports

ITG's range of Best Practice Reports is now at *www.itgovernance.co.uk/best-practice-reports.aspx*. These offer you essential, pertinent, expertly researched information on a number of key issues including Web 2.0 and Green IT.

Training and consultancy

IT Governance also offers training and consultancy services across the entire spectrum of disciplines in the information governance arena. Details of training courses can be accessed at *www.itgovernance.co.uk/training.aspx* and descriptions of our consultancy services can be found at *http://www.itgovernance.co.uk/consulting.aspx*. Why not contact us to see how we could help you and your organisation?

Newsletter

IT governance is one of the hottest topics in business today, not least because it is also the fastest moving, so what better way to keep up than by subscribing to ITG's free monthly newsletter *Sentinel*? It provides monthly updates and resources across the whole spectrum of IT governance subject matter, including risk management, information security, ITIL and IT service management, project governance, compliance and so much more. Subscribe for your free copy at: *www.itgovernance.co.uk/newsletter.aspx*.

CPSIA information can be obtained at www.ICGtesting.com
Printed in the USA
LVOW081326101111

254387LV00006B/3/P